The Border Outlaws
An authentic and thrilling history of the most noted bandits of
ancient or modern times: the Younger Brothers, Jesse and
Frank James, and their comrades in crime

James W. Buel

# TABLE OF CONTENTS

# PREFACE.

An authentic history of the desperate adventures of the four Younger Brothers has become a necessity. Their lives require no romantic or exaggerated shading to make the narrative remarkable. Their deeds are as prominent in the archives of guerrilla warfare as their names are familiar on the border. But with a comprehension of the morbid appetites of many readers, newspaper and pamphlet writers have created and colored crimes with reckless extravagance, and then placed upon them the impress of the Younger Brothers, because the character of these noted guerrilla outlaws made the desperate acts credited to them not improbable. The difficulties encountered in procuring facts connected with the stirring escapades of the outlaw quartette, have heretofore been overcome by imaginative authors and correspondents, giving in minute detail incidents with which their creative genius is at all times well supplied. These remarks are not intended to disparage the merit of any contributor to the annals of border history, but rather to excite a proper suspicion on the part of the public against a too ready belief of every adventure, fight or robbery charged to the Younger Brothers.

The part they acted during the great civil strife has, undoubtedly, been truthfully told, but their career since the close of that dreadful drama has been, in a great measure, elaborated by imagery, until it is difficult for those unacquainted with the facts, to conclude which record is true and which created.

The writer does not claim exception from mistakes, but without arrogating to himself any special merit, it can be truthfully said that the following history of these great outlaws contains a less number of errors and a more reliable and comprehensive description of their valorous deeds than any previous publication. For several weeks prior to the completion of this work, a correspondence was maintained with the Younger Brothers, as well also with the warden of the Minnesota penitentiary, and through this source many new facts were obtained and numerous errors discovered. In addition to this, personal interviews have been had with several old comrades of the Youngers, and with Cole Younger himself; and nothing has been left undone to procure all the facts possible, and to avoid falling into the old mistakes which have been repeated until they have become almost traditionary.

For a considerable period the writer was a resident of Kansas City, where he was engaged in journalism, and made the acquaintance of hundreds of persons who were intimately known to the Younger and James Brothers, and from these also much valuable and trustworthy information was received, which various corroborative sources have enabled the author to reliably write the history of the noted outlaws without resorting to either fiction or romance.

J. W. B.
St. Louis, December 15, 1880.

# NATIVITY, AND CAUSES WHICH LED TO GUERRILLA LIFE.

Henry W. Younger, father of the outlaws, was one of the early pioneers of Missouri, having removed to the State in 1825 and settled in Jackson county. Five years later, having arrived at manhood's estate he was married to a Miss Fristo, a very estimable young lady of Jackson county, and the relation thus formed was a congenial and happy one. Mr. Younger, possessing a fair education, became a prominent citizen in the neighborhood and for the period of eight years he held the position of County Judge, and subsequently was twice elected to the State Legislature. The family became a very large one, consisting of fourteen children, eight of whom are still living, four boys and four girls.

In 1858 Mr. Younger purchased a large tract of land in Cass county, near Harrisonville, to which he removed the same year and began raising stock, in which he was eminently successful and soon became a wealthy man. He made many excellent investments which finally caused his removal to Harrisonville, where he started a livery stable and became interested in two large country stores.

Thomas Coleman, familiarly called Cole, was the second eldest son, having been born in Jackson county January 15th, 1844.

Richard was the senior of Cole by two years, but he died of a malarial fever in 1860 before the exciting events which culminated in a career which has made the family name so prominent.

John was born at the old homestead in Jackson county in 1846, Bruce in 1848, James in 1850, and Robert in December, 1853. It is not important to give the births of any other members of the family, as their names will not figure in the incidents herein recited.

It is not surprising that western Missouri has produced so many remorseless characters, considering the peculiar conditions of her early history. Every student of common school history is familiar with the border warfare which existed between Missouri and Kansas over the slavery question. Old John Brown, whose career terminated at Harper's Ferry in 1860, was an important factor in that inter-state contest which was waged with almost unexampled fury for many years, to the destruction of a vast

9

amount of property and the loss of hundreds of lives. The border counties of Missouri and Kansas suffered terribly from the incursions of "Jayhawkers" and "Border Ruffians," afterward guerrillas, as the opposing factions were called; and perforce Col. Henry Younger was involved in the bitter antagonism, as was every property owner in that section.

One of the incidents of the bloody border warfare has been immortalized by the Quaker poet, John G. Whittier, and its reproduction here will serve as a more forcible illustration of the desperate cruelties inflicted in that contest which lighted the camp-fires of Abolitionism and prepared the way of freedom for Southern slaves.

The history of this local event so elegantly and pathetically apotheosized by Whittier is in brief as follows. In the year 1856 Hamilton, whose reputation for fiendish brutality had preceded him, drew his serpent trail across the border and appeared in Miami and Linn counties, Kas., at the head of about fifty conscienceless followers. He pillaged and burned farm houses, laid waste teeming harvests and murdered men, women and children of anti-slavery opinions. The crowning act of his career was the arrest of twenty of the best citizens of Linn Co., all residents of a single neighborhood, whom he bound and carried to a lonely spot on the Marais du Cygne river, near Trading Post, and securing them to stakes, fiendishly shot them one by one. Three of the number, though wounded in a manner which gave evidence of their death, survived to tell the terrible story of that holocaust and become heroes of Whittier's verse. Two of the survivors are still living, or were during the writer's residence in Kansas in 1872. One of these. Rev. Reed, is pastor of the Baptist church at Ossawatomie, Miami county, and the other, Asa Hargrove, is a prosperous farmer of Linn county.

Such, in brief, are the particulars of that dreadful sacrifice so passionately wreathed with pathetic garlands by one of America's greatest poets, and many a tear has fallen from the eyes of sympathetic readers upon the pages which relate the story. Following is the poem:

### LE MARAIS DU CYGNE.

A blush as of roses
Where rose never grew,
Great drops on the bunch-grass,
But not of the dew!
A taint in the sweet air

For wild bees to shun
A stain that shall never
Bleach out in the sun!

Back, steed of the prairies!
Sweet song-bird, fly back!
Wheel hither, bald vulture!
Gray wolf, call thy pack!
The foul human vultures
Have feasted and fled;
The wolves of the Border
Have crept from the dead.

From the hearths of their cabins,
The fields of their corn,
Unwarned and unweaponed,
The victims were torn, —
By the whirlwind of murder
Swooped up and swept on,
To the low, reedy fen-lands.
The Marsh of the Swan.

With a vain plea for mercy
No stout knee was crooked;
In the mouths of the rifles
Right manly they looked.
How paled the May sunshine,
O Marais du Cygne!
On death for the strong life,
On red grass for green!

In the homes of their rearing,
Yet warm with their lives,
Ye wait the dead only,
Poor children and wives,
Put out the red forge-fire,
The smith shall not come;
Unyoke the brown oxen,

The ploughman lies dumb.

Wind slow from the Swan's Marsh,
O dreary death-train.
With pressed lips as bloodless
As lips of the slain!
Kiss down the young eyelids,
Smooth down the gray hairs;
Let tears quench the curses
That burn through your prayers.

Strong man of the prairies.
Mourn bitter and wild!
Wail, desolate woman!
Weep, fatherless child!
But the grain of God springs up
From ashes beneath,
And the crown of his harvest
Is life out of death.

Not in vain on the dial
The shade moves along,
To point the great contrasts
Of right and of wrong;
Free homes and free altars,
Free prairie and flood, —
The reeds of the Swan's Marsh,
Whose bloom is of blood!

On the lintels of Kansas
That blood shall not dry;
Henceforth the Bad Angel
Shall harmless go by;
Henceforth to the sunset,
Unchecked on her way,
Shall Liberty follow
The march of the day.

At the beginning of hostilities in 1861 the border warfare increased in virulency and the sympathizers on both sides were forced into extreme measures. Col. Younger, though it is claimed he was a Union man, suffered terribly from the Kansas militia, who were operating under the Federal banner. Jennison, who was at the head of the jayhawkers, made a raid through the counties of Jackson and Cass, leaving behind him a trail of burning farms and plundered villages, staying his hand of desolation in the town of Harrisonville, a large portion of which he destroyed; among the property he confiscated was all the livery stock of Col. Younger, consisting of thirty head of horses and several buggies and wagons. This act was bitterly condemned, but there was no other means of compromising the wrong than by avenging it upon the people of Kansas.

From this time the members of the Younger family renounced their Union sentiments and enlisted their sympathy with the Confederate cause. A few weeks afterward Cole Younger sought and found Quantrill, whose force he joined and pledged himself to the fortunes of that dreadful black banner which two years afterward streamed through the bloody streets of Lawrence.

# COLE YOUNGER'S FIRST FIGHT UNDER QUANTRILL.

Three is no reason to doubt Cole Younger's assertion that he joined Quantrill because of outrages perpetrated by jayhawking Federals upon his father, and it must be admitted that he did not renounce his manhood by so doing. It was terrible to see the property of the household confiscated, and other indignities suffered at the hands of those whose banner should have made them friends. Cole Younger was a young man of excellent character, refined by education and a training which made him devoted to his parents. Little wonder, then, that his nature became transformed by such cruelties upon those he loved so well, and when he allied his fortunes with the most desperate man on the border, it was the preliminary step in a determination to have revenge.

When Cole Younger volunteered his services Quantrill's force had but recently been collected and consisted of thirty-seven men, all of whom were residents of Jackson, Clay and Cass counties. For several weeks this small company confined its adventures to the border counties of Kansas, taking horses and capturing ammunition trains. Capt. Peabody, with a full company of Federals, was sent out by Gen. Jim Lane, who was in command of the Kansas militia, with instructions to capture or kill Quantrill and his band. The trail was readily found and the guerrillas were followed to the house of John Flannery, in Jackson county, where a stand was made January 3d, 1862, and a bitter fight ensued. The Federals surrounded the house and then sent a demand to Quantrill for his surrender. The cunning guerrilla asked for a ten-minute parley with his men, which time being granted, he used it most advantageously in disposing his men so as to make them most effective. At the expiration of the time allowed, Quantrill shouted defiance at his foes, at the same moment discharging his double-barreled shot-gun, which was loaded with buck-shot, killing Peabody's lieutenant. The fight then began in earnest and for more than an hour it raged with increasing fury. Finding it impossible to dislodge the enemy by pouring shot into the building, Capt. Peabody ordered the torch applied to the house, an act easily accomplished in the rear of the ell of the building, as there were no windows from which an approach from that direction could be commanded. A large quantity of straw was carried from an adjacent stack which, being fired, soon enveloped the frame ell, but ere the flames reached the main buildings they were quenched by the guerrillas. A second attempt resulted as the first, but the water in the house now being exhausted, the third time fire was set to the building it roared and crackled like a fiend of destruction to be baffled no more. Smoke rolled through the windows and the hot flames came leaping into the rooms, driving the guerrillas from corner to corner and rapidly narrowing the space they stood on until, at last, they were forced to face their foe and stem the torrent of death without protection. By orders of Quantrill, dummies were hastily made of pillows and bed clothing and set in the windows to draw the fire of the Federals, and then bidding his men follow, the desperate guerrilla dashed through the door and broke for the brush, every man emptying his gun at the enemy as he ran. Cole Younger displayed the most remarkable bravery throughout the fight, and at the retreat his recklessness caused him to separate from his command, and but for the operation of what seemed almost a miracle, he must have been killed. Being unacquainted with the place, Cole ran in a different direction from the others of his command and suddenly found his course impeded by a strong picket fence which he could not scale, while the Federals dashed after and fired at him more than a hundred times. After running fully two hundred yards, with a large force in pursuit, he came to a defective place in the fence, and pushed through and started across a field. But, though he had distanced the infantry, there were twelve cavalrymen who saw him, and to tear down the fence was the work of a moment and then the pursuit was renewed. Cole still carried his gun but it was empty, he having had no opportunity to reload, but from time to time he would raise the gun as if intending to fire at his pursuers, and this act would serve to partially check their rapid ride after him. By recourse to such strategies Cole gained the woods and escaped, most singular to relate, without having received the slightest wound.

In this fight the guerrillas lost ten men, but two of these refused to leave the burning building and therefore perished in the flames. The loss of the Federals was eighteen killed and nearly as many more wounded. None of the guerrillas were captured but all their horses fell into the hands of the victors.

# THE DESPERATE FIGHT AT TATE'S HOUSE.

The Flannery fight was repeated with remarkable similarity one month after that occurrence. The particulars of this combat, as related by Geo. Shepherd, a participant, to the writer, are as follows: At this time Quantrill's force consisted of exactly fifty men and was on the march towards Sny-Bar, where it was learned a small detachment of Federals were operating. It was Quantrill's custom, while on the march, to stop at farm-houses on the way, distributing his men so that their accommodations might be provided for. While enroute for Sny-Bar, night coming on, Quantrill, with twenty-one of his men, stopped at the large farm-house of Major Tate, near Little Santa Fe, in Jackson county. The rest of the company, under Todd, found lodgings five miles further north.

Hard riding had made Quantrill's men weary, and a fast since morning had whetted their appetites into unusual cravings. Major Tate was a friend of the cause, and a bounteous table, set with all the good things provided by a successful farmer, was the welcome he extended to his guests. Without there was snow and whistling, frosty winds, while within was the crackling log-fire with its reflection of dancing images and warming cheer; hunger-producing odors of fresh meats smothered in rich gravies; smoking sweet potatoes, and the luscious condiments which a thrifty housewife had provided for special occasions; in addition to these seductive refreshments to the hungry there was the brown cruet of freshly drawn cider with its crest of breaking bubbles, and a pyramid of apples red as the cardinal's robe. It was supper time, and such a lordly feast the guerrillas had not partaken of for many months.

After supper was over, every man, with distended stomach, uncomfortable from excessive fullness, gradually became languid until sleep stole upon them in spite of the good jokes which were passing around and being told with special zest by the jolly Major.

The guerrillas were asleep, all save one who stood sentinel at the gate, his big coat muffling his face from the biting gusts of winter's winds. Slowly he paced a little beat, his dreamy eyes closing, at times, with fading resolution, but only to open wider when full consciousness was restored. Nine, ten, eleven o'clock, and not a sound to disturb the deep slumbers of the guerrillas. The hour of midnight was approaching, that mysterious time when the dead are permitted to catch glimpses of the earth they once trod in the flesh; that period of brief space when graves open to disgorge their surfeit of dead men, and on which the shadows fall which margin the confines of death and life. Were these gloomy reflections occupying the dreamy mind of that lonesome guard; he who was called to slay and spare not; to hunt, to find, to kill?

"Who are you?" The clock was striking the mysterious hour, and the food for graves was being prepared, but the graves had not yet been dug. It was the voice of the guard who, startled by the tramp of horses' feet in the crisp snow, gave the guerrilla challenge, and as the road filled up with Federal cavalry there was a single shot, and a rush by the guard into the house. A volley from carbines saluted his entrance, but the door was speedily barred against intruders. Cole Younger, Geo. Shepherd and Quantrill heard that first shot and intuition told them its full meaning: the enemy was without, two hundred strong, and a fight was unavoidable. Some one was always on Quantrill's trail and the force which had now surrounded him had followed his track like a sleuth hound, and only waited for the deepest shades of night to fall upon and devour the little guerrilla, band. The Federals understood the cunning and bravery of the twenty-two men in the building, and before making their presence known they had taken every precaution to prevent escape, by completely surrounding the house and guarding every door and window. The night was beautiful, with the sky as clear as the ether of heaven, from which a full, bright moon poured a flood of silver, pencilling the white earth and throwing dark, fantastic figures behind the woods and fences.

A brave lieutenant was the spokesman of the Federals, and with clanking spurs and saber he approached the door, gave it a few smart kicks with his heavy cavalry boots, and then demanded an immediate surrender. It was a moment when there was no need for orders; every guerrilla understood his duty, for sleep is easily dissipated in moments of extreme danger. Quantrill strode cautiously to the door, and, locating the lieutenant by his voice, fired a large navy pistol. The bullet cleft through the panel and struck the officer in the chest. With a gurgling moan the lieutenant fell, and with a few convulsive struggles died. The battle then began, with the Federals pouring volley after volley into the buildings which, though it was weather-boarded on the outside and had a filling of brick between the studding, yet it afforded but slight protection against the minie balls that were poured into it. The guerrillas were divided, with Quantrill, Cole Younger and six others in the second story, while the first floor was occupied by Geo. Shepherd, Quantrill's lieutenant, and the remainder of the force.

After the fight had progressed for a short time four of the guerrillas became so frightened that they wanted to surrender, and it also became important to extend some special protection to Major Tate and his family. Accordingly, Quantrill hailed the Federals and told them some of his men desired to surrender, and that the family of the house wanted protection. Permission for them to retire was therefore given and the four guerrillas, followed by Maj. Tate, much against his will, and his family, left the house, taking up quarters in the barn which stood some distance off. The fight was then renewed. Cole Younger, with the same reckless bravery which distinguished him at the Flannery fight, took desperate chances and did terrible execution. The snow became crimson in many places and the cries of the wounded fretted the air. Time and again came the summons to surrender, but the only reply was a scornful laugh. It was thus the combat continued for three long, terrible hours. No one had yet thought of the torch, though there was the same fatal ell with no window to guard it, as at Flannery's. It came, though, at last, and when the flames threw their lurid glare in through the crevices of the barricaded windows the guerrillas realized how near grim fate was approaching. Time was asked for, but the Federals refused to check their fire until terms of unconditional surrender were agreed to. Quantrill, in last extremities, always proposing some desperate scheme, ordered all his men to stop firing and reload. When every pistol and gun was heavily charged, the guerrillas massed themselves, threw open the two doors and leaped upon their foes, pouring an unceasing volley into the Federals, cutting a bloody gap through which they passed to safety.

Singular to relate, though none the less true, the guerrillas, besides losing their horses, had only one man killed, and none wounded. The Federal loss was a score killed and nearly twice that number wounded. A junction was formed the next day with Todd, and in a skirmish with thirteen Federals which occurred in the afternoon following the Tate house fight, horses sufficient were captured to remount Quantrill and his men.

# THE SLAUGHTER AT BLUE CUT

From the time of the fight at Major Tate's house the guerrillas changed their methods of retaliation, and a fighting campaign was inaugurated which ceased only with the close of the rebellion. The militia of Missouri co-operated with the Federal forces of Kansas, and every highway in the border counties became a battle ground. Quantrill's force was augmented by recruits from neighboring counties, accessions being made at every camping place. Their arms consisted of such weapons as the new recruits brought with them or captured from routed foes. Horses were readily obtained by forage upon stables and pastures, while ammunition reached them through the secret avenues of sympathizing friends.

After his escape from Capt. Peabody's cavalry, Cole Younger went to the house of Jerry Blythe, a relative, located on the Independence and Harrisonville road, and staid there two days before he could learn the whereabouts of Quantrill, whom he was anxious to rejoin. The Federals stationed at Independence learned of Cole's appearance at Blythe's, and a force of seventy-five mounted troops at once started out to effect his capture. News of the Federals' intention reached Cole and Quantrill, and a plan was immediately arranged to intercept and give them battle, while a courier was dispatched to acquaint Mr. Blythe with the purpose of both Federals and guerrillas.

By direction of Cole Younger Quantrill's force, now numbering fifty men, was stationed at a place called the Blue Cut, on the Harrisonville road, fifteen miles from Independence, through which the Federals would have to pass on their march, or make a circuit of five miles by a bad road, to reach Mr. Blythe's house. The cut is about twenty-five feet in depth and of a width that will admit of the passage of not more than two wagons, while both sides of the summit are lined with a heavy forest in which it was an easy matter for Quantrill to secrete his horses and men.

For some reason, doubtless to prevent the knowledge of their appearance in the neighborhood, the Federals chose the circuitous route and reached the Blythe mansion unperceived by the guerrillas. They found no one at home except Mrs. Blythe and a young son not more than thirteen years of age, who was in the yard when the Federals rode up. They captured the young lad and tried to force him to disclose the hiding place of Cole Younger, but he positively refused to tell anything; and when they gave him a chance he ran into the house, seized a pistol, and while the troops were sacking the place he fired on them, killing one and severely wounding another. This unexpected attack from so youthful a source so enraged the Federals that, as the boy ran out at the back door, he was riddled with bullets, no less than sixteen striking him, extinguishing his young life immediately. After the commission of this deed and being satisfied that Cole Younger was not in any of the outbuildings, the Federals started back on the main highway, when they were soon seen by the guerrillas and preparations were at once made by the latter for the attack. Both ends of the cut, as well as the eminence on each side, were well protected by the guerrillas, whose fire was reserved until the unsuspecting Federals had ridden well into the gap. With a wild yell from Quantrill the work of destruction was begun, and the murderous streams of flame made the cut a hideous valley of death. From every side the deadly pellets poured upon the demoralized Federals, not one of whom thought of anything but escape, while horses and riders mingled their blood together until that terrible gap became red with the slaughter. Few lived through that destructive fire, for when the whirlwind of death swept over the band, nearly sixty corpses lay still under the smoke which choked the cut. Cole Younger's avenging hand had been laid heavily upon ten men, and he was satisfied with the work of that day.

# THE MOST REMARKABLE FIGHT DURING THE WAR.

In the latter part of February, 1862, three weeks after the slaughter at Blue Cut, one of the most remarkable battles of the war was fought, between Quantrill's force of fifty men on one side and five hundred Federals under Cols. Buel and Jennison on the other, resulting in the defeat and rout of the latter with a loss almost twice as great as the entire guerrilla force.

Independence had become a supply post and distributing center for the Federals in the west, and was garrisoned by a force of one thousand militia. Spies were continually on the track of the guerrillas, but owing to the disbandments and reorganizations which occurred every few days to avoid pursuit, it was impossible for the Federals to determine the force of the enemy in any engagement, which gave to Quantrill a most important advantage.

In the latter part of February, the weather being very cold, Quantrill went into camp on Indian Creek, in Jackson county, about ten miles from Independence, for the purpose of recruiting his force and watching the movements of the enemy. His position was soon reported and Col. Buel, at the head of two hundred men, at once drew out from Independence for the purpose of engaging the guerrillas, whose numbers were found to be small. By some means, never fully explained, Quantrill suffered himself to be surrounded, though his defensive precautions were excellent; a large number of trees having been felled and breastworks made which no cavalry could penetrate.

On the morning of the 26th, Quantrill was surprised by the shrill whistle of a shell as it came cutting through the trees and exploded overhead. His pickets were driven in and then he found that every avenue of escape had been closed, besides which the Federals had two pieces of artillery with which to shell the woods. The situation was critical in the extreme and Quantrill had grave apprehensions which he communicated to his comrades. At the suggestion of Haller, a brave fellow who saw the anxiety manifested by Quantrill, Cole Younger was called into council because of his thorough knowledge of the country and the cunning and daring which had already distinguished him. His advice, undoubtedly, saved the command and turned what at one time seemed certain defeat and inglorious surrender, into the most brilliant victory of guerrilla warfare.

Cole communicated to Quantrill the fact that inside the Federal lines was a large farm-house with adjacent yards filled with cattle. His advice, therefore, was to hold the enemy in check until night, make every indication of a stubborn resistance, and then stampede the stock, which would confuse the Federals, draw their fire and make escape possible. His suggestions were at once received with the greatest favor and, for the time being, he was practically placed in command of the force. All day the fighting was continued, but the loss of the Federals was quite severe, while the guerrillas suffered slightly, owing to the excellence of their fortification, and the difficulty of throwing shells through the heavy growth of timber. When night approached, the guerrillas made active use of the axe in felling more trees, ostensibly to strengthen their position, but in reality to deceive the Federals, and the ruse was successful. The night was one of unusual darkness, as there was no moon and the heaviest clouds banked the sky. Out into the gloom crept Cole Younger, William Haller, Dave Poole and George Todd, four men whose hearts never harbored fear, and in a few minutes after they left the quiet camp a terrible confusion was heard in the barn-yard; chickens were cackling, dogs barking, and in the noise a score of affrighted cattle were heard running and bellowing, their speed being accelerated by several pistol shots, which brought the Federal camp to arms in the belief that the guerrillas were upon them. The cattle were mistaken for foes and a lively rattle of musketry told how successful had been the strategy of Cole Younger and his aids.

The confusion resulting from the stampede and the darkness permitted the guerrillas to withdraw from their beleaguered position and when morning broke they were in the rear of the Federals ready to make a bold stroke, which had already been agreed upon. Quantrill knew the position of the battery and that the line could hardly withstand a determined assault at any point.

When the dawn came Quantrill followed Cole Younger in a desperate charge upon the surprised artillerymen, and the battery was captured with the least show of resistance. A large force of cavalry, under the command of Jennison, was seen rapidly approaching at this instant, and as they wheeled to the right for the purpose of forming a junction with Buel's infantry the latter officer mistook Jennison's force for Col. Upton Hayes, Confederates, and the greatest disorder was at once developed. Quantrill took advantage of the mistake, and in a moment he dashed among the demoralized infantry and turned loose the captured battery upon the now thoroughly routed foe. Seeing Col. Buel's infantry cut to pieces Col. Jennison concluded that the Confederates, or guerrillas, were massed in large numbers and that it was discretion on his part to withdraw. But he was not permitted to escape the fire of the guerrillas, who turned from the pursuit of Col. Buel's panic-stricken command and directed their guns upon Jennison. His cavalry never having been under fire before, were soon thrown into disorder, the horses being stampeded by the shells and whistling bullets, and but for the protection of a friendly corn-field the havoc would have been terrible. The victory, however, was complete, resulting in a loss of one hundred Federals, a large number of horses, twelve hundred rounds of ammunition — an ammunition train being at the time escorted by Col. Jennison — and a battery of two ten-pound guns. The loss of the guerrillas was only eight men. The cannon were spiked and then thrown into the Big Blue.

In this battle the remarkable fortunes of war are manifested. The Federals were as brave and commanded by as good officers as were the guerrillas, but the strategy which first permitted the latter to escape, and the determined charge, followed by a mistake on the part of the Federals, placed them almost at the mercy of the guerrillas. It is little incidents which often win battles, not always bravery or larger forces.

# HISTORY OF THE BLACK FLAG.

The circumstances which created the black banner and made it the in hoc signo of the guerrillas, have never been related in history, important and interesting as they are. The facts which are herewith recorded were obtained from Geo. Shepherd, than whom no other man now living is so competent to give the truthful particulars.

Living in Lafayette county, Missouri, in the summer of 1862, was a family by the name of Fickle, consisting of the old gentleman, whose first name Shepherd has quite forgotten, his wife, and a daughter, twenty years of age, named Annie. The family were all of intense Confederate predilections, but while the old gentleman contented himself with giving expression to his opinions only among his immediate friends, his daughter was virulent and overt in her sentiments and sympathies, which caused her father no little solicitude, for in those days men were killed for opinion's sake.

In May, one of Shepherd's guerrilla comrades was found in the house of Mr. Fickle, by a company of Federals, and was arrested. The guerrilla was a particular friend — perhaps a lover — of Miss Annie's, and when the arrest was made she became so abusive to the Federals that she was also taken into custody and carried into Lexington, where she was imprisoned for a week, and then permitted to return home.

The guerrillas were very anxious to secure the release of their comrade, whose fate, if not averted by some special means, they could readily anticipate. To accomplish this Shepherd called on Miss Annie, through whose influence with a Federal lieutenant, who was her cousin, he hoped to procure an exchange of prisoners that would liberate his friend. Annie forthwith placed herself in communication with her lieutenant cousin and finally appointed a meeting between Shepherd and the Federal officer. At this meeting the lieutenant agreed to effect the release of the captive guerrilla for the sum of $400, which being consented to, another appointment was made for the succeeding night, at which the money was to be paid and the captive would be at a certain place to which they would ride and meet him.

Shepherd had not entertained the slightest suspicion of treachery because of the supreme confidence he reposed in Miss Annie. True to the engagement, he met the lieutenant at the trysting place shortly after nightfall, and together they rode to the spot indicated. After passing several miles they came to an angle where the road they were traveling united with another. At this point on one side was a stone fence and on the other a large pile of brush. As the two approached the brush-pile about twenty Federals arose from the ambush and fired on Shepherd, killing his horse which, in the fall, pinioned one of his feet for a moment, but as horse and rider fell, Shepherd drew his pistol and killed the lieutenant, whose treachery was then apparent. By extraordinary efforts Shepherd released himself and darted for the stone fence, which he leaped amid a shower of bullets, and, being fleet of foot, ran rapidly along and behind the fence until he had outstripped his pursuers, who groped aimlessly in the dark, not being able to discover which direction Shepherd had taken.

Three weeks after this narrow escape, and two weeks after the execution of the captured guerrilla, who was shot. Major Blunt, commanding the post of Independence, (Shepherd is not certain, but believes Blunt was in command at the time, and that he was also the author of the order), issued an order which he caused to be printed in the Independence paper, to the effect that from the given date, guerrillas captured would not be treated as ordinary prisoners of war, and that all parties found bearing arms against the United States of America-, in the district specified in the proclamation, would be regarded as guerrillas and punished as such. The inference gained from reading the order was that thereafter all guerrillas or armed forces opposing the United States would, in case of capture, be executed. The purpose of the order was, no doubt, to prevent by intimidation, the recruiting of Confederate companies in Jackson county, and hardly contemplated the harsh and cruel methods which inference had attached to it, for it was never put into execution.

A few days after the issuance of this order, while Quantrill and his company, of about sixty men, were camped near the little church in Sny-Bar township, the pickets reported the presence of Annie Fickle, who desired an audience with the command. She was, of course, admitted and her mission was to make a presentation. Under her left arm she carried a bundle wrapped in a newspaper, and in her left hand there was a strong, smoothly polished hickory pole. Annie, though born where nature was rugged in the wilderness of its untrained productiveness, was nevertheless of a romantic temperament. Plain of speech, she was, notwithstanding, gifted with lofty sentiments, and it was these she had gathered that day and arranged in a bouquet of fervid enthusiasm. Giving a courteous bow to Quantrill, she asked him to have his men assemble for a moment around her. Her request being complied with, she unrolled the bundle and taking the paper which bound it, she read Maj. Blunt's order of "death to all guerrillas," then in a brief harangue she addressed the men in language, nearly as can be remembered, as follows;

"It is a hard fate which awaits every brave Southern soul found in Missouri fighting for a cause as sacred to every true man as is the love of God. To falter now, is to betray the holier instincts of love and liberty, and in the peril which this infamous and bloody order imposes upon the noblest sons of Missouri, I can see rising this oriflamme, (shaking out the folds of the black banner), which, though black as death, is purified by the righteous cause it represents. Life to life and blood for blood; let the border ring with the cry of freedom, Quantrill and the sunny South, one and indivisible forever, and to you, into whose hands I entrust this banner, let me nerve you with my prayers and entreaties never to lower it so long as there is a hand to clutch the staff, or until the principles of the Confederacy are decided by the sword and bayonet, when there is no longer hope for appeal.

"And ever let your battle-cry be,
Quantrill and Southern Supremacy!"

While making this little speech Annie unrolled the black banner, which had been carefully bound up in the paper containing Blunt's order, and spread it upon the grass. When her remarks were concluded, she produced a hammer and nails and fastened the flag to the hickory pole in a dozen places.

The banner was made, by Annie's own hands, of quilted alpaca, four thicknesses, and its dimensions were three by five feet. In the center was deftly worked, in sombre colored letters, the name "Quantrill," running endwise through the middle of the flag. The pole was eight feet in length.

The donation was received in a demonstrative manner of approval, the men lifting their hats and giving three cheers for Annie Fickle, while Quantrill thanked her heartily and promised to carry and protect the banner so long as he had life to do it Jim Little was chosen color-bearer, and he bore it conspicuously, though not in every combat, until after the destruction of Lawrence. The flag was carried with Quantrill to Kentucky in 1864, torn as it was by a hundred bullets, and disappeared with the guerrilla band in their last fight. Its remnants may still be preserved by some Kentucky relic lover, but if so, its owner is not known to Shepherd.

# THE PILLAGE OF OSCEOLA.

Following the fight at Indian Creek came the pillage of Osceola, in St. Clair county, by Jim Lane. This act, though unaccompanied by horrors like those which distinguished the Lawrence raid, was equally as indefensible. Osceola was a flourishing town of about one thousand inhabitants whose peaceful homes were not disturbed or threatened until the jayhawkers came down upon it like a wolf in the night and applied the torch to every building of any consequence in the place. By the light of the destroying flames stores were plundered and many outrages perpetrated upon the defenseless citizens. It was the result of savage and dishonest natures relieved of all legal restraint and encouraged to exercise their vandalism and thievish bents by unscrupulous and equally criminal officials. Osceola became the war cry of the guerrillas for years afterward, and to this day when the stigma of Lawrence is pointed out to the Younger Brothers they never fail to refer to Osceola as the prime cause for that dreadful holocaust.

# THE SECOND FIGHT AT THE BLUE CUT.

Cole Younger was appointed second lieutenant in Quantrill's command in April, 1862, and thereafter the squad fighting by guerrillas was begun. In June information reached Quantrill that a company of fifty men, under Capt. Long, was on the Harrisonville and Independence road, foraging on the route to the latter place. Cole Younger was given a detail of twenty-five men and ordered to ambush the detachment of Federals at the Blue Cut, an order which he executed with what success will appear. From spies sent in advance Cole learned that among the Federals was a former guerrilla by the name of Shoat, who had enlisted under Quantrill a few months previously and then deserted, carrying with him valuable information for the enemy. Cole had harbored the suspicion that Shoat, was a spy and he therefore became specially anxious to kill him. Capt. Long, however, was an old acquaintance of Cole's, and in earlier days the two had been boyhood friends, little reckoning how destiny had linked them to antagonistic causes in the desperation of guerrilla warfare.

Having posted his men advantageously so as to sweep the cut with a galling fire when the Federals should enter, Cole spoke to his comrades and begged of them, under no circumstances, to kill Capt. Long, whom he thoroughly described, but at all hazards not to allow Shoat to escape.

It was about three o'clock in the afternoon of June 12th when the Federals rode into the cut unsuspicious of any lurking danger, when suddenly a volley from twenty-six pistols dissipated the good humor of that unfortunate command and a fight to the death was begun. Capt. Long was a man of extraordinary nerve, and by his heroic words and bravery rallied his surprised force and notwithstanding his disadvantage he stood for a time like a stone wall, giving shot for shot. The guerrillas, however, fought from the summit of the cut and it was therefore impossible for the Federals to reach them.

Fifteen minutes of desperate fighting, with the havoc all on one side, caused a stampede and the demoralized Union forces dashed over their dead and wounded comrades in determined effort to escape, despite the entreaties of their commander. When the rout became general Cole Younger ordered a pursuit in which he shot Capt. Long's horse from under him, and then, espying Shoat, he gave chase and at the second fire from his heavy pistol shot the deserter in the back, breaking the spinal cord, from which death resulted in a few moments. Cole then rode back to Capt. Long, who had been made a prisoner, and greeted him in the same cordial manner as if the two had met after a long separation under happiest influences and unsevered friendship. A few moments were spent in conversation, after which a list of the dead and wounded was made, and then the prisoners, numbering ten, including Capt. Long, were released on parole. In this sharp fight the Federals lost twenty-seven killed and wounded, while the guerrillas suffered the loss of only three men killed and five wounded, one fatally.

# THE BATTLE OF WALNUT CREEK.

In July, 1862, Quantrill's command had been increased to seventy-five men, an addition of twelve men having been made by a union with Jack Rider who had been ravaging the border counties on his own account. With this force Quantrill decided to make a retreat from the Sny hills and enter Harrisonville, which at this time contained a large amount of provisions guarded by about one hundred raw Federals. His designs were frustrated, however, by his advance guards reporting large bodies of scouting militia on every side. The roads were, in fact, so well protected by the Union forces that Quantrill was forced to take to the woods, and even this course did not exempt him from pursuit, for his trail was followed persistently and being unable to throw the enemy off his track he was compelled to retrace his steps and make for the Sny again.

After several days of hard marching, Quantrill pitched his camp on Walnut Creek, in Johnson county, which he fortified by felling heavy trees and making his retreat inaccessible to cavalry except at passes left for the convenience of his own troops. Cole Younger was sent out on the 13th of July to reconnoitre and forage, taking with him twelve men well mounted. Upon reaching the house of Joe Larkin, a detachment of fifteen men was espied riding up the road in advance of a large force of Federals. Cole and his men had dismounted and their horses were feeding back of the house. Hastily calling his squad together, he ordered them to hide behind some quilts, which had been washed that day and left on the fence to dry. Thus secreted, they awaited the approach of the Federal advance, until they were in the road immediately opposite, when suddenly the guerrillas arose as if from the ground and poured such a deadly fire upon the fifteen astonished Federals that but one escaped. The main body was so surprised at this sudden and fatal attack upon the advance-guard, that it halted and formed in line of battle in anticipation of a charge, as the Federals had no idea of the guerrilla force. At this juncture an additional force of two hundred Butler county militia appeared, and thus reinforced, the Federals advanced while Cole mounted his men and retreated to the camp, where preparations were made to receive the enemy. There was no delay, for Quantrill had scarcely time to close the passage through which Cole Younger and his squad had entered, before the Federal cavalry, now four hundred strong, made an impetuous charge, but they recoiled before the murderous fire of the well-protected guerrillas. A second charge followed, led by as brave men as ever rode in battle, but again from the barricades streamed flames of death until the brook which babbled along the base of the hills was gorged with the dead. The baffled and distressed cavalry fell back in broken ranks and formed on a hill two hundred yards distant, evidently to hold a council. For two hours not a sound disturbed the stillness of the forest. The two armies were content to quietly contemplate the intentions and strength of each other. In the afternoon, about four o'clock, the Federals were again reinforced by another body of two hundred men, and the attack was renewed. A force of one hundred deployed down the creek and another detachment of two hundred was sent to attack the guerrillas in the rear, but the bluffs prevented the latter force from reaching a point where they could be effective. A combined attack was agreed on, but when the charge from the front was made again, the main body was unsupported by the three hundred troops sent to attack the flank and rear, and a terrible repulse was the consequence.

The several disastrous charges made by the Federals convinced them that the cavalry was useless against such a strongly fortified foe, and a new plan of attack was resolved upon. All the troops were dismounted and their horses secured in the ravine five hundred yards north of the battle-ground. The combined force then moved in infantry columns, and with solid phalanx ascended the hill, reserving their fire until the last moment. The sight now was a grand one. The guerrillas, with double-barreled shotguns loaded deep with slugs and buck-shot, lay low behind their barricades and waited the approach of the enemy. Not a gun was fired, nor a word uttered until the Federals had almost reached the sheltering works and were preparing to scale them, when suddenly there was a rattling peal which shook the sleeping forest and a cry of anguish arose which converted that spot into a place too horrible for nature. The line wavered under that mortal fire, but the rents were repaired in the attacking column, and the onset continued. It was almost a steady stream of deadly fire that poured over and through the crevices of the fallen trees and the havoc was too terrible for the bravest to stand. Despite their exposed position the Federals fought with a valor never surpassed; though their ranks were melting away like a thin depth of snow before a warm sun, yet the survivors were men of steel and fought like heroes battling for life. Notwithstanding the protecting butts of large trees, the guerrillas suffered severely. Quantrill was shot through the leg, but still he fought and cheered his men while the blood ran away and wasted his strength; Cole Younger had his clothes riddled with bullets and his hat shot off; Geo. Shepherd was hit in the arm, and more than a dozen of Quantrill's men were lying here and there, in pools of their own blood, never to fight again. To render escape more difficult, nearly half of Quantrill's horses were killed and the country was almost as thickly beset by large bands of scouting Federals as with trees, brush and lofty bluffs.

The charging forces were four times beaten back from the impregnable barricade, tottering under the flying pellets of death, but rallying again and again until the dusky shadows of evening obscured foe from foe. The roar of battle ceased gradually and when the smoke uplifted nothing relieved the painful quiet which succeeded save the shrill piping of summer insects and the distant monotone of a soliloquizing owl.

Late in the night Cole Younger, with two others, was sent out to locate the enemy for the purpose of ascertaining the safest avenue of escape. Quantrill's wound was now giving him much pain, his fighting; force was seriously crippled and his ammunition almost exhausted. To remain and risk the battle which was certain to be renewed on the morrow, he realized would be sure defeat followed by the most disastrous consequences.

Directly after Younger and his two comrades left the camp to reconnoitre a heavy rain began to fall which, rattling among the trees, permitted them to proceed with less fear of detection and indisposed the Federal pickets to keep vigilant guard, for they were already fairly exhausted from fighting, and naturally sought shelter and rest.

It was nearly twelve o'clock, midnight, when the daring spy returned and made his report to Quantrill. Cole had crawled inside the Federal lines, located every squad and picket, and then found a clear passage, but it was up a dreadfully steep hillside which only the surest footed animal could climb. But even this information was encouraging, and hurriedly yet silently the camp was raised, the wounded mounted with aids, and the tattered ranks of the guerrillas were put in motion. It occupied more than an hour's time to get the horses and men up the hillside, and in the confusion the Federal camp was aroused to Quantrill's intention. The darkness, however, was friendly to the guerrillas and protected them in their escape, many of them being compelled to ride double, owing to the scarcity of horses. The Sny hills were reached, the wounded were left at the houses of friends, and hastily separating the trail was broken.

# AMBUSCADES AND HARD FIGHTING.

Quantrill and Shepherd received the best surgical attention, and as their wounds were slight they soon recovered sufficiently to resume active operations.

Before calling the command together, however, Cole Younger and George Shepherd were sent into Kansas City with instructions to procure all the ammunition possible, while Quantrill went to St. Joseph to collect arms. The guerrillas being life-long residents of the neighborhood in which they fought, had many valuable friends who gave important aid in all their undertakings. It was not difficult to procure munitions of war in Kansas City, and in two days after entering the place a goodly store was secured, which was loaded into a wagon and the two guerrillas started back to the appointed rendezvous on the Sny. Five miles from the city they put up at a friend's house for the night, but before bed-time they were surrounded by a body of Federal cavalry who, by some means, learned of Younger and Shepherd's visit to Kansas City and had been placed on their trail by spies. Back of the house was a field of wheat almost ready for the harvest, and in this the wagon was secreted, while the horses were larriated between two out-buildings, ready for emergencies which were anticipated. The Federals demanded an immediate surrender, accompanying the order with a threat to fire the house in case of a refusal. The position, critical in the extreme though it was, induced no thought of capitulation. Looking out of the windows the guerrillas discovered where the guard was weakest and drawing their revolvers they rushed out of the back door, killing four men as they ran, and gained their horses in a shower of leaden rain. Both were struck, Cole being hit with three balls, which produced only flesh wounds, however, while Shepherd was shot in the shoulder and thigh, which prevented him from keeping his horse, after riding a few hundred yards. Younger succored him with true comrade sympathy and under the cover of night the two made good their escape, and again Shepherd was given over to the care of friends until his wounds should heal.

Younger, seeing his friend provided for, bandaged his own wounds and then joined Todd on the Big Blue, where, on the following day, with a squad of fifteen men they fell on the flank of a Federal scouting party

35

which they routed, killing six of the number. Three days after, the same guerrilla force came upon an ammunition and supply train under the convoy of fifty Federal cavalry in the eastern part of Johnson county, Kansas. The meeting occurred on the banks of the Aubrey, and, fortunately for the guerrillas, they found the enemy powerless, owing to their intoxicated condition, as with the train were several barrels of whiskey. The attack was a slaughter as of helpless brutes, not a Federal escaping, and the atrocities of the murder are shocking to remember even now. Men were shot down and then bayoneted, their riddled carcasses being left to fester in the summer sun. The supplies captured were taken to the retreat in the hills, more than compensating for the loss of the wagon left by Younger and Shepherd in the wheat field.

Five days later, Todd and Younger with their destructive squad of fifteen, met nineteen Federals as they were crossing the Big Blue, in Jackson county, in a hand ferry-boat. Awaiting until they were near the shore on which the guerrillas were secreted, such a deadly fire was poured into the thoroughly surprised Federals that not a single one escaped.

These fatal surprises made the Union forces more cautious and determined. Spies were sent out to locate the guerrillas and an ambush was planned into which Todd and Younger rode without a suspicion of danger. Their cruel tactics were being played against them, and had the Federals exhibited the remorseless nature of their enemies, not a guerrilla of that band would have been left to tell how desperate was the assault near Stoney Point.

The place selected for the ambush was a rugged spot on the road between Pink Hill and Stoney Point, about one mile from the latter place. There was a shallow cut in the road and on each side was a heavy timber of oak and hickory, and many large rocks which afforded the most secure hiding-place for an enemy. The squad rode leisurely into the enfiladed passage with Younger and Todd at the head of the column, who were chatting humorously together about their recent escapades. Suddenly, right ahead of them, they heard a shot and quickly following was a rattle of rifles and the whizz of bullets cutting through the guerrilla ranks, emptying several saddles and demoralizing even those who had faced death frequently before, when it stalked in their midst in more hideous aspect. The guerrillas dashed through the guarded road and with rare good luck escaped destruction. The Federals had not made the most of their opportunity. The first fire was given before the guerrillas were fully in the passage, owing to the accidental discharge of a gun which gave warning to the guerrillas, and compelled the Federals to deliver their fire prematurely. In addition to this mistake, instead of resorting to the destructive revolver and furiously charging the guerrillas after firing their carbines, the Federals waited to reload and this gave the enemy time to recover and return the fire, after which they dashed off towards the Blue with one hundred and twenty-five cavalry in hot pursuit. The chase continued for several miles, Todd and Younger hoping to reach Quantrill, who had reported his return from St. Joseph with a large number of navy revolvers and one hundred carbines. When they reached the bridge over the Blue, on the Kansas City road, the situation became more complicated, for directly in front of them, Todd and Younger, who were in advance, discovered a body of mounted Federals whose carbines and sabres glistening in the sunlight, bristled with preparation for murderous work. Enemies behind and in front, more than twenty times their own number, caused the bravest heart in that little band to sicken with gravest apprehension. There was no time to hesitate, it was of all others the moment for spontaneous action. The charge was ordered at the enemy in front, but what could so small a force do against overwhelming numbers in an open fight? They fell back under the burden of that galling fire, with Younger's horse shot from under him; Todd's clothing cut to pieces; Martin Shepherd killed, and Blunt, Yaeger and Bledsoe desperately wounded. Wheeling his horse, Todd shouted encouraging words to his comrades and Younger, with a pistol in each hand, fighting in his desperation, shouted to the band to follow him, and dashing toward the bank of the stream, which rose perpendicularly more than five feet, he leaped into the water followed by those on horseback. They crossed under an ineffectual fire and, with Younger mounted behind Todd, the shattered squad rode through the brush and gained Quantrill's retreat in the Sny hills.

# THE FIGHT AT INDEPENDENCE.

Col. Upton Hays had been among the Sny and Blue hills for several weeks recruiting a Confederate regiment, and had collected a force of six hundred men. Having now the most effective arms and a good supply of ammunition, Quantrill sought an interview with Col. Hays, and the result was a determination to attack Independence, which was garrisoned by five or six hundred Federals, under command of Col. Buel. One of the prime motives of the intended attack was to accomplish the deliverance of about thirty Confederates and guerrillas, who had been captured and were then confined in the Independence jail.

To prepare for the fight, by locating and fixing the strength of the Federals in the immediate neighborhood, which might be available for reinforcements to harass his retreat, if such a movement became necessary. Col. Hays selected five of Quantrill's bravest men, Cole Younger, Yaeger, Miller, Young and Muir, and with these, made a detour of observation, clothed in Federal uniform.

When the squad reached Westport, they found the place held by twenty-five of Jennison's men against whom the guerrillas had sworn vengeance and a fight of extermination. In their uniform disguise. Col. Hays and his men had no difficulty in entering the place without molestation. Finding the jayhawkers unprepared for an attack, Yaeger shot one of the guards, which became the signal for a slaughter. At the first volley four of Jennison's men fell dead, and before the others gained their arms more than a dozen more were killed or wounded. One specially obnoxious German was chased to his house by Cole Younger, the door broken in, and in another moment his dead body was dragged into the street by Younger, who shouted: "Here is food for buzzards!" The remaining jayhawkers had now reached the cover of buildings and procured arms. It was time for Col. Hays and his uninjured men to retreat, which they did, galloping down the road rapidly only to find the way obstructed by a body of fifty cavalry. A blind lane turned to the right and into this the squad dashed, bringing up suddenly against the fence with fifty sabers and carbines in their rear. Fortunately, for fortune seemed to favor the guerrillas, the fence was not very high and the rails rotten; it was therefore easy for men so used to the saddle and desperate extremities to leap the barrier and fly over the field to safety. Much valuable information was gained by the detour, but the most important knowledge concerned Independence; how the forces were stationed; the strategic points in the place; the location of the jail; the exact force of the garrison and the preparations to resist attack from every side. Who should gather this information? Upon whom the service would devolve was determined with the query, for who was so well adapted to such dangerous adventures as Cole Younger? Who so fertile of resource, so cunning in conversation, so perfect in disguise? Cole was selected to perform the dangerous mission of a spy, and, with all its attendant perils, he was as happy in such a recognition of his abilities as a school boy with his merit mark.

Left to his own judgment, Cole procured an ancient, home-spun linsey-woolsey dress, in which he had some alterations made to better accommodate his person. Next in importance was an old faded sun-bonnet with yellow strings and broken pasteboard stiffening. His feet he encased in men's gaiters, which were split up in the center to give them the appearance of women's shoes; a rough wig with hair combed closely down over his temples, completed the personal outfit. For conveyance he rode a horse in whose eyes lingered an unchangeable disposition to sleep, but in his heels there was the speed of a hurricane. The saddle was for a man, which, in that section of country, performed duty for male and female members of the family alike. The bridle was comical to look upon. It had originally been a blind-bridle, but now one of the blinds had fallen off; the throat-latch was a tow string, and the curb was of home-spun woolsey, while rope and tow strings held many of the broken parts of the bridle together, and a piece of sea-grass rope answered the purpose of reins.

Thus attired, with a large covered market basket on his arm, Cole Younger rode into Independence on the main highway. The pickets gave no heed to the ancient backwoods grandmother, and Cole rode up into the public square, where, after hitching his horse, he spoke kindly to many of the soldiers and gave them large red apples from his basket. A crowd of soldiers gathered around him, to whom he gave all his apples and then began a conversation as follows:

Said Cole, changing his voice to a tone suitable to his appearance: "I am nothing but a poor old woman with few years before me, but I've lived under this government a long time, and, do you know, I can't think about the effort that is now being made to destroy it, without crying. You see, old folks don't like to change, and they are always anxious for their children to enjoy all the good things they have enjoyed."

"Where do you live?" interrupted one of the soldiers.

"I live out near Pink Hill, about ten miles from here, right in a nest of the worst rebels in fifty miles of the Sny. Quantrill has been laying around there for these two months past; has stolen all my chickens, taken the best hoss I had, and poor Johnnie, my baby, only fifteen years of age, he carried away and flogged him almost to death because he was my child and Union to the core."

"Where is Quantrill now?" asked a soldier, evidently much interested in the old woman's honest and pathetic story.

"Why, he's outen there somewheres about now, and I tell you, if I had two hundred brave men, old woman as I am and got no sense, I'd tackle Quantrill if it was the last act of my life."

This patriotic ebullition brought forth several expressions of "good!" "good!" from the interested squad around her. One of the men then asked the old woman if she knew anything about fighting.

The reply was: "Well, nothing to speak of except what I inherited; I used to be purty lively with my finger-nails when I was a young gal; we used to have some high times, you know, at corn huskin's and quiltin's, and I've seed the hull crowd gouging and clawing wuss'n a pack of wild cats, and I was reckoned one of the most vigorous in the pack too."

The crowd laughed and joked the old woman about her pluck, and then asked her if she knew how to handle a rifle or revolver.

"I used to a leetle, but my eyes haint good any more, and I don't think I could knock a squirrel's eye out from the tallest branches of the big hickories around here, any more, but twenty year ago I could."

After some further joking on the old woman's prowess, she changed the subject back to Quantrill.

"Well, what I'd like to know is, if the Federals about here can't kill that Quantrill and his cut-throats, and save our property. How many men have you got in this here place, anyhow, and how are you fixed for fighting?"

The soldiers responded: "We've got nearly six hundred men here, but then we can't leave the place to pursue Quantrill, for if we did, the Rebs might turn on us and capture Independence."

"What good would it do them if they did? wouldn't you be doing better service by killing the infernal and thieving Rebels, than by staying in here doing nothing?" responded the old woman.

"Yes, but then you should remember, we have a large amount of government stores here; powder, rifles, provisions, etc., which might fall into the hands of the Rebels if we left them unprotected," was the soldier's reply.

"Well, I don't know nothing about war," remarked the old woman, "but I'd like to be edecated on it a leetle. This is the first time I've been in Independence since the troops took the town, and I'd like to see what you all fight with and how you live; where you keep your prisoners; how many you've got, and, in short, jist how the hull thing is done."

The soldiers very courteously told the old woman where the jail was, and that she could go all around the place and look at everything she pleased.

The road was now clear to obtain what information was desired, and at every point where anything special was needed. Cole would engage some soldier in conversation and successfully obtain full explanations.

About five o'clock in the evening, having made a thorough inspection of every spot in the town. Cole returned to his horse, which he backed up to the fence and mounted. He rode slowly out of town but upon approaching the outer picket a sergeant, seeing the covered basket on Cole's arm, and being suspicious that it contained some medicine or arms for the enemy, as such smuggling was common, ordered the picket to halt and examine the old woman. Cole tried to parley with the picket, but finding all entreaties vain, and knowing the results of an investigation, instantly drew a pistol from beneath the folds of that ancient dress, and ere the guard anticipated the movement a ball went crashing through his brain. Cole then threw his right leg in proper position in the saddle, gave his drowsy horse a jerk, which threw the lightning into his heels, and away he sped followed by three mounted soldiers who, however, were soon distanced, and the daring spy reached Quantrill and Hays in safety.

In the gray of the morning of August 11th, 1862, Hays and Quantrill with a combined force of over seven hundred men, nearly all of whom were, however, raw recruits, led by the intrepid Younger, attacked the camp on the west side of town with a cavalry charge. The first picket was killed and the Federals surprised, though they were not demoralized. The roll was quickly beaten, Col. Buel dashed the sound slumber of the morning from his eye-lids, and the line of battle was formed with extraordinary celerity. The guard fired on the swiftly approaching enemy and then retired in good order to the buildings. Nearly every picket was killed, but when Hays and Quantrill poured their troops into the public square they met with a reception little expected. From every window there were puffs of smoke and red flames. Hays was compelled to dismount his men and seek the protection of walls and fences. He then attacked the camp while Quantrill struck at Buel in the houses. But he had a force to contend with that was steel to steel. Hays carried the camp and then joined Quantrill in the onslaught against the building occupied by Buel and a hundred of his men. Muskets and revolvers could not dislodge them, but fire could. A farmer's wagon, loaded with hay, stood in the square, and this was drawn along-side of the doomed building and set on fire. The swift flames shot upward and their malignant tongues soon licked the cornice and roof, eat up the shingles and fastened on the rafters. Superhuman exertions and consummate bravery could not extinguish fire guarded as it was by death dealing carbines and revolvers. Buel fought like a tiger at bay until the fierce heat scorched his face, and to hold out longer meant death too terrible to meet. The white flag had to be unrolled and flung to the breeze, and Buel, the bravest of the brave, was forced to capitulate unconditionally.

After the capture came the pillage. The wounded were cared for, and the dead, which lay around the square, were buried, after which all the prisoners in the jail were liberated, the Federals paroled and the stores confiscated. The price of victory and defense was great, more than one hundred Confederates being killed and wounded, while the loss of the Federals was fifty-seven.

# THE BATTLE OF LONE JACK.

Jackson county had become an active volcano, pouring down from its sides searing lava and filling every village, hillside and valley with woe. It was the fighting and recruiting ground of guerrillas, Confederates and Union men, neighbor against neighbor, schoolmate against schoolmate, and war to the knife. Every rivulet had a bloody tinge, every home its victim.

Five days after the capture of Independence came the dreadful fight at Lone Jack, a hamlet in Jackson county, twelve miles from Independence, consisting of two country stores, a saloon, blacksmith shop and a dozen other buildings.

Col. Joe Shelby, Col. Ward Cockrell and Col. John T. Coffee, each at the head of a few hundred men, had come into Missouri from various points, all with the same intention, to recruit their respective commands and then begin an active campaign through Missouri and Arkansas, and drive Gen. Curtis out of the former State, who was doing the Confederate cause much damage. The three commands formed a junction two miles north of Lone Jack, and went into separate camps on the evening of Friday, August 15th. By a singular coincidence Major Emory Foster, a brave and able officer in command of one thousand Federal cavalry and supported by two pieces of artillery, entered Lone Jack on the same night and went into camp. Maj. Foster's purpose was to strike Quantrill, who was located by Federal spies in that section, not for a moment anticipating a meeting with a full regiment of regular Confederates.

The few residents Lone Jack contained were in full sympathy with the South, and word was speedily communicated to the Confederates of the Federal's proximity, their strength, equipment, etc.

Cockrell and Foster had, at one period of their lives, been residents of Warrensburg, and the former knew that in the fight which could not be avoided, nothing but good luck and brave men could save him. Long rides had jaded the Confederates' horses and a rest was necessary; this was the reason an attack was not made during the night, but this excuse is hardly pardonable under the circumstances, when the advantages of attacking an enemy, unconscious of lurking danger, are so conspicuous and invaluable.

Quantrill would scarcely have waited until the camp had become quiet, ere he would have plunged in, heading a charge like the mad dash of ocean breakers and irresistible as the lightning's bolt. But Quantrill was not there, neither was the intrepid Shelby, for on the morning preceding the battle he had departed for Waverly to meet a force of Confederates awaiting him. But leading the troops by platoons were Jackman, Tracey, Rathburn, Hunter, Bohannon, Hays and Coffee, the latter, however, being too far to the south (where, with nearly two hundred men he was scouting) to participate in the fight.

Col. Cockrell had command, and shortly after receiving the report of the Federals' position he called his men to arms and formed in line of battle on the main highway to Independence, one-half mile from the enemy's outposts. The line of battle was maintained for nearly an hour, when it was decided to break ranks, sleep on their arms and make the attack early in the morning. This action of Col. Cockrell has been severely criticised by Confederate officers but criticism is no part of faithful history, and comments and conclusions are therefore left for the reader. Cockrell's bravery, it is but proper to add, never was nor can it be questioned, for it was thoroughly tested in the battle of which we write.

Lone Jack lay sleeping in the prairie, with a cornfield and heavy hedge rows on the east side, and a growth of timber lined the murmuring brooklet which curved a half-circle of the town on the west. In the place was a two-story frame building called the Cave House, an old-fashioned country inn. This house was Foster's headquarters, and from an upper window floated the stars and stripes. The hamlet took its name from a large and lone black-jack tree which stood like a solitary sentinel at the apex of a prairie knoll, two hundred yards south of the Cave House, but like many of those who fought around its trunk on the 16th of August, it is now in the process of decay.

At four o'clock in the morning the Confederate bivouac was raised and the hurry and bustle of preparation for the early battle was begun. The horses were placed in charge of a guard of fifty men, and the regiment, consisting of a few less than one thousand men, was disposed, by orders of Col. Cockrell, as follows: Jackman, with a force of three hundred, was stationed near the steam mill south of town; Tracey, with a like number of men, took up a position in the cornfield east of town, while Bohannon stretched his line on the south-west with instructions to drive in the pickets and the first shot should be the signal for a combined movement and general attack. When the positions were taken it was not yet day, but the eastern portals of light were flecked with an aureole of beautiful red, signaling the approach of a cloudless day.

It was six o'clock before the quiet of early morning was broken by the signal gun, much unnecessary delay having occurred, and before the attack was begun, the Federals had discovered the enemy and were ready for the onset. When Tracey's line advanced rapidly, expecting to meet a surprised foe, ere he reached the limits of the town, a raking fire was poured into his astonished ranks, which caused much confusion, but his men soon rallied. Tracey, however, was shot in the foot and had to be taken from the field, but his place was quickly filled by Hunter. Jackman and Bohannon were slow in coming up, but when they struck the enemy's flank, they drove the Federals from the hedge rows, and the fire from three sides soon drove them into the buildings.

The artillery could not be made effective because of the proximity of the Confederates, and the fire which drove the gunners back under shelter, and after a most desperate and stubborn fight the guns were captured. At this juncture. Cole Younger, with forty mounted guerrillas, hearing the fighting, came dashing into the rear and reported to Col. Cockrell. Cole was sent into the action without any delay, and the fighting grew hotter. Maj. Foster, seeing his artillery in the hands of the Confederates, and being planted beside the blacksmith's shop where it could batter down his defences, rallied his forces, and placing himself at the head of three hundred men, swept down upon the enemy with such resistless fury, that the Confederates were forced to retreat and permit the Federals to recover the guns. From this time Foster forced the fighting and the hand-to-hand encounter in the street became terrible. A hundred men held the hotel, and from their position did dreadful execution, killing Captains Bryant and Bradley, and preventing, for a long time, the approach of the Confederates up the street. Something had to be done and that quickly; it was either a retreat or drive the enemy from the hotel. Cole Younger was the first to suggest fire, but who so rash as to drive through the fatal hailstorm of bullets and apply the torch? The answer came from the guerrilla hero. Turpentine balls were a part of the guerrilla's equipment, and at the head of a dozen men, ten feet apart. Cole rushed through the deadly volleys and flung the burning balls in and against the building, leaving half his men dead in the effort, but escaping himself unhurt. The dreadful scene before became appalling now. The roar of crackling flames mingled with the rattle of musketry and the death cry of victims. Driven from that furnace of destruction, the Federals poured out of the doomed building, shooting as they ran, but few lived to find another shelter. Among the slain was the lady of the house, who fell, pierced with a dozen balls, on the very threshold; bullets are no respecters of persons; it was her misfortune and the regrets of the Confederates could not infuse life again into that innocent and bleeding body. Driven from the buildings, the Federals fought with the fierceness born of desperation; the streets were fairly choked with the dead; hand to hand and hilt to hilt, saber and bayonet, pistol and gun, blood for blood, and thus the fight continued for more than three hours. Younger was here, there, everywhere; the keen crack of his pistol was the cradle which harvested death.

The fight progressed with the Federals giving way inch by inch, and moving slowly southward, which was now the only by-way of escape. Maj. Foster was wounded in six different places, and Capt. Foster, his brother, shot to death; still the brave Federals would not yield so long as there remained a fighting force. At noon, when the hot sun beat down upon that field of carnage and the exhausted, sorely stricken Major saw the bloody heaps of his fallen comrades, and the few brave men of his command, battling against hope, it was only then that he yielded, brave even in the last act. In this terrible battle the Federals lost two hundred killed and more than five hundred wounded, and the Confederates suffered a loss somewhat greater. Two hundred of Foster's men made their escape and reached Lexington four days after the fight, while those captured were paroled and sent to their homes.

# ASSASSINATION OF COL. HENRY W. YOUNGER.

On the 20th of July, 1862, Col. Henry W. Younger, father of the Younger Brothers, was waylaid and assassinated, five miles from Independence, while driving in his buggy towards Harrisonville. He had a large sum of money on his person at the time, being the proceeds of a sale of cattle made in Independence the previous day. When the body was found, the pockets were turned inside out, about four hundred dollars having been taken. The assassins, however, failed to find the larger sum, several thousand dollars, which Mr. Younger had placed in a belt he wore around his body beneath his underclothes.

Cole Younger was soon made acquainted with the tragic death of his father and at once returned home to be present at the funeral services, regardless of the danger encountered in so doing. It was reported that the assassins were Jennison's Red Legs, but of this there is no proof, though Cole harbored suspicions, and he never rested until the last person whom he suspected of complicity in this crime was dead, and his revengeful hand murdered not a few.

Mrs. Younger was naturally a very delicate woman with the hectic flush of consumption coming and going in her cheeks. Trouble, which laid its hand heavily on her when the eagles of war spread their pinions, gave food to the insidious disease and melancholy marked her for its own. Cole looked into the dear eyes of his anguished mother and the revenge in his bosom was bent even against nature, to lift that dreadful burden from off her precious heart. James and John were almost ready to join the banner of the prairie vulture, but there were sisters, and her whose support had just been broken, needing protection, and desire for revenge could not break the seal of duty. The property of the family had been greatly wasted by foraging parties of jayhawkers, who had come to regard Cole Younger as the incarnation of atrocity and murder, and were determined to punish the family for his crimes. Not a week passed but the house of Mrs. Younger became the objective point of a squad of militia or jayhawkers in seach of Cole. Indignity after indignity was perpetrated and the most cruel means resorted to in the endeavor to extort information of his whereabouts. It was thus the horrors of war fell athwart the Younger's household, making the very air they breathed pestilential.

# SKIRMISHES, AMBUSCADES AND EXECUTIONS.

In the latter part of September, Quantrill's forces were called together for the purpose of reorganization. The policy of the guerrillas was to fight, disband and reorganize; cemented in their fellowship by oaths and obligations, whether separated or united their hearts and arms were ever ready to respond to the needs of their cause. When the winding horn reverberated through the forests it was Quantrill's call to the rendezvous, and when the roll was read every name responded with a cheerful "on duty." One hundred and twenty men, well armed and mounted, were ready to begin active offensive operations against militia, pillage unguarded posts, capture provision trains and kill — kill — kill. The guerrillas rode out of Missouri to leave their bloody trail through Kansas, and make reprisals of men and chattels. At Shawnee Quantrill found a half-hundred undrilled militia who surrendered to him without firing a shot; two miles below there, on the route to Olathe, seven mounted men were captured, and ill was the hour of their birth, for the decision was that they belonged to Jennison's band. That decision meant quick death. To his men, "bring the ropes;" to the captives, "pray," were all the words spoken by Quantrill. Among the number was a young man, only a lad in fact, with black eyes full of courage. He had but one request to make: "Let it be the rifle instead of the rope," and the last wish of his life was granted. From a broad-reaching oak limb six bodies hung side by side among the dying autumn leaves, and at the root of the tree one face looked upward into the unknown with the stare of death in his eyes.

From Shawnee the guerrillas sped on to Olathe, twenty miles further south, where they captured seventy-five more militia, men unused to war, who never thought of resistance; they performed the part of a sham battery, or, like sentinels of straw, to intimidate only by appearances. All these were paroled, and after feeding their horses and appropriating needful provisions, Quantrill turned to the east, passing through Aubrey and over ground made familiar to him by previous expeditions.

Reaching Cass county, in the northern part, the guerrillas learned of a convoy of one hundred and fifty Federal cavalry with ten heavily loaded wagons of government stores, enroute to Kansas City. It was the time for an ambush. The pick and shovel, in many expert hands, soon made convenient rifle pits along the road and then, secreting their horses back in the woods, the guerrillas patiently awaited the approach of the cavalry. Quantrill was on the left, Todd on the right, and Younger in the center of the ambushing file. It was on the 2nd of October when the doomed convoy came slowly up the road with the wagons in the center, creaking under the heavy loads. On each side of the road there appeared nothing but the natural stillness of the woods. For a hundred yards the trenches extended along the highway and the command was given not to fire until the convoy had ridden abreast the complete line of the pits. There was breathless silence, as every man resolved himself into an engine of destruction, pausing, like a tiger, before the death spring on its victim. Unconsciously the train wended slowly along over the road of bloody fate, the men laughing, singing love songs, passing jokes, talking of loved ones at home and repeating stories of Quantrill's deeds of murder. When the convoy came abreast of the ambushed line, without a word of warning, the gates of hell seemed to open on the left, and over the sides of the masked trenches poured a stream of flame, smoke and lead, starting at the lower end of the line and running its length, like a trail of powder touched by a spark. It was a work of murder, the surprise was so complete, and as dead men fell with the autumn leaves, fire was applied to the wagons, and the terrors of that seething hell were thus multiplied. More than seventy of the Federal column lay in the highway with only heat from the burning train left to give them burial. The rest of the convoy broke with the first fire and by desperate riding reached Kansas City.

The woods were now resonant with the crack of the rifle, and human game was easily found by the opposing forces. Every hillside was a redoubt, every ravine a rifle-pit; a foe seemed lurking behind every tree and death held his revel in the border counties.

The Harrisonville and Kansas City road was a principal highway along which Federals, Confederates and guerrillas were daily traveling. The ample preparations made at the slaughter-pits were too advantageous to be readily abandoned, and on the following day it was decided to hold a second carnival at the same place. Accordingly, the guerrillas took up a position in the commodious trenches, while Cole Younger, Gregg, Geo. Shepherd and Scott, were sent out to deploy down the road and, if possible, decoy another body of Federals inside the masked dead line. Several hours elapsed ere there were any indications of a "find," and the patience of the anxious ambuscaders was becoming restless. Dave Poole rose up from his sitting posture in the pits and putting his hands behind his ears, to better catch the sound waves, waited a moment, and then in a low voice asked:

"Did you hear that shot?"

"No, from what direction?"

"A little to the west, I think," was the reply.

"There! three more in quick succession. Boys, they have struck them, sure!"

Poole and Quantrill then put their ears to the ground.

"Look out, they are coming on a dead run, for I can hear the clatter of horses' feet," remarked Quantrill.

"Get ready, every man, it's a chase, for they are firing on the retreat."

Sure enough, there was a pursuit, the sound of horses feet, and the rattle of pistols and guns could not be mistaken. On they came at the bent of their speed, the pursued, with nearly two hundred Federal cavalry thundering in their rear, not two hundred yards behind. At the pits there was a quick turn in the road and, hidden for a moment from the charging cavalry, the four intrepid decoys dashed into the woods behind the trenches, leaped from their horses and rushed to the slaughter which had now begun. A sheeted flame broke from the pits as the Federals breasted the line, and horses and riders plunged into the dust, while the air was rent with cries of the wounded and made stifling with powder smoke.

But the fight did not end with the first volley, for, although fifty saddles were emptied, the Federals quickly comprehended the situation, and with reckless bravery, dismounted and began an onslaught on the works. Fighting from behind trees, on the flank, front and rear, the carbines did dreadful execution. Within an hour the Federals were reinforced by Col. Hubbard's Sixth Missouri cavalry, of three hundred men, and then the tables of death were turned on the guerrillas. A desperate charge was hurled against the entrenched enemy, which swept up to the very muzzles of the guns, but a tornado of bullets hurled back the column and left the ground strewn with dead men. Hubbard's bravery was equalled only by the fanatic martyr.

"To the front, Charge!" again came the command, and again the blue line advanced with fixed bayonets into the very face of the guerrillas, but again that sheet of flame burst from the trenches and the stricken Federals trembled, then fell back in confusion. Charge after charge was made, but each time repelled by that storm-burst of leaden hail. It was folly to fight longer against such disadvantages. Night had approached, but the round, full moon and a star-decked canopy lighted up the battle-ground, and Col. Hubbard, unwilling to give up the contest, fell-back for the purpose of surrounding the guerrillas and holding them until the morrow. His intention was, however, anticipated and the ambushers drew off at the first opportunity, carrying their wounded with them, and retreated into the Blue hills where they camped and rested for two days. In this engagement the Federals lost nearly one hundred killed and the guerrillas twenty-two, and as many more severely wounded.

After resting and receiving several new recruits Quantrill divided his men into squads and sent them in different directions to harass the Federals and confuse his pursuers. Younger, with twelve men, took the route toward Little Blue, and it was not long before he had work for his revengeful hands. At a bridge, over Little Blue, the guerrillas met a mounted squad of twenty Federals and the passage had to be made by one party over the dead bodies of the other. To meet an enemy meant a furious charge to Younger, and his tactics were put into execution at the bridge. Giving the enemy no time to consider, Younger shouted "to the charge," and at the head of the hurricane he rode into the ranks of the Federals, shouting and slashing like hunters in a herd of buffalos. Two alone of the twenty escaped, each because of some favor shown Younger in earlier days, and not one of the guerrillas was even wounded.

But fortune did not always favor the fierce fighters, for the Federals multiplied, and to slay a detachment was like killing flies in summer time, the number seemed undiminished. Pressed on every side, confronted in every road and by-way, driven from every shelter, the guerrillas began to tire; squad-fighting was too dangerous, the pursuing forces of the Federals too numerous, and Quantrill again ordered a meeting at the old rendezvous on the Sny. Every man was there whose body was intact; some there were in the garrets of their friends' homes, with wounds like church doors; others were bleaching in public roads, in lonely ravines, or sleeping in the noisy woods — noisy not with the melody of plumed warblers, but the crack of the carbine and clash of the saber. Some came to the trysting, bleeding from bullet sores that had not yet healed, and when the roll was called again there were still more than a hundred names on the list ready for duty.

Peabody, Burris, Hubbard, Jennison, Montgomery, Anthony and a score of others had entered into a war which thought not of the subjugation of the

South, only the annihilation of Quantrill and his terrible band. On the first day after leaving the rendezvous, Quantrill met the foe; with the first discharge of pistols and bullets his enemies multiplied by a rush of reinforcements. The retreat was a running fight through Jackson, Cass, Johnson and a dozen other counties. There was no time to cook or forage, except as they gathered on the constant watch. Younger, Shepherd and Gregg became the reliance of Quantrill, without these he could have done nothing but surrender or fight, and fighting die with empty pistols in his grasp. These three men, whose unparalleled heroism was their armor, rode in advance or to the rear, wherever their services were most needful, now checking a pursuit by some clever strategy or discovering an ambush, gathering forage for the horses and food for the men, they were the fortune and succor of Quantrill's army.

Near Wellington the guerrillas met three score Federal militia in the highway, and with the first sight came the cry from Younger to "charge." The retreat which the militia sounded only helped the slaughter. A few fired at the avalanche and the intrepid Scott was struck badly in the thigh, but he did not leave the saddle. On, on the charge swept, and when the contact became too close for the pistol the saber took its place; cuts to the right, left, and thrusts to the front, the fleeing ranks grew thinner until not a life was spared, and strung along the road for four miles were bleeding corpses, the only product of that retreat.

Wheeling to the right to avoid a large force of Federals in the front, Quantrill crossed streams, burning bridges behind him, breaking the trail by riding in branches, and using every precaution to elude pursuit; still he could not rest. Foes were everywhere and no strategy could steer him clear of destined tribulations, fierce fights and disastrous results. Between the Sny and Big Blue, with retreat to the rear prevented by destroyed bridges, Quantrill rode into the clutches of Col. Burris, a brave Kansas Federal, with three hundred men. There was but one way of escape, and that lay in a desperate fight, with the chances three to one against him. Desperate extremities can best be met by desperate acts, and Quantrill was the first to sound the charge with Younger, Shepherd, Todd and Gregg in the advance. Col. Burris was in the valley while Quantrill was coming down the hillside in that wild, impetuous, running sweep so irresistible that when he struck the solid Federal column the momentum broke Burris' ranks and left a bloody gap, but at such dreadful sacrifice to the guerrillas that out of nearly one hundred two-thirds of them were killed and hardly a man got through without a wound. Quantrill was hit in the shoulder, George Shepherd, Harrison, Todd, Poole, Gregg, and in fact all the best fighters except Younger were wounded more or less severely. The stroke was too heavy for the guerrillas to bear and maintain their organization, and another total disbandment became imperative, every man able to ride selecting his own method for escape. Many hid for days in caves among the bluffs of the Sny, whilst others moved like shadows, at night, through the forests, and slept like bats in the hollow of trees and other dark shelters during the day. It was thus that the campaign on the border closed in 1862.

# THE SEPARATION AND COMBATS IN DIFFERENT FIELDS.

Quantrill with a few followers, bade farewell to Cole Younger and started south to join Shelby and renew the campaign where the winds of winter blow like mild and cooling zephyrs, and where pinching frosts never visit to bite and wither the sweet smelling verdure of the evergreens and magnolias. Cole Younger remained to scout and watch in Jackson and Cass counties. He was not long quiet, for the charm of guerrilla life, like the odors of the poppy, lured him back again into the old paths consecrated by the sacrifices of direful war. Gathering together a dozen farmer boys, who had escaped the conscription of Federals and Confederates, he first taught them how to ride and shoot, and appealing to their softer sentiments in the inspiriting words of chivalry and patriotism, made of them knights of the highway exalted with an ambition to fight and kill. To get them into practice, Younger led them into ambuscades from whence mail couriers were shot, and lone travelers, suspected of Union sentiments, were cruelly massacred. They soon learned to smother their conscience, and then to fight small squads caught foraging on barns and granaries. The force gradually grew larger until on the first of December Younger found himself at the head of twenty-five amateur guerrillas, which number was further increased by a union with Todd, who returned from the south with fifteen men. The company was again ready for active service, though no important engagements took place until January, 1863.

The militia were constantly in search of Younger; baffled in their efforts more than a hundred times, they became desperate and resorted to desperate expedients. A Federal force of fifty men went to the home of the Youngers, in Cass county, and surrounding the house in which they felt certain Cole was secreted, made a rush, and with cocked guns and drawn swords were ready to kill and quarter their victim. A diligent search failed to discover Cole, but that the long ride from Independence might not prove entirely fruitless, three of the Misses Younger were placed under arrest and carried to Kansas City, charged with aiding and concealing their guerrilla brother. They were confined in an old guard house, which being undermined by rats and natural decay, during a high wind was blown down, and in the fall two of the sisters were killed and the other seriously injured.

The arrest and death of his sisters converted the cruel guerrilla into a veritable fiend, and made Cole Younger as voracious for blood as the hungry tiger. Who can say that his revenge, if not entirely satiated, was not terrible to contemplate? but, to his credit let it be recorded, he never killed a woman.

About the middle of December, Younger and Todd made a trip into Kansas for the purpose of collecting horses and fighting detachments of Jennison's men, who were reported as operating at various points in companies of fifty and one hundred. Scarcely had they entered Wyandotte county, ten miles from Little Santa Fe, when they met a force of jayhawkers, numbering sixty, and a fight was the result. It was on the open prairie, and bringing into execution the old tactics of the guerrillas, a charge was made, in a swift run, with a pistol in each hand, and the bridle-rein in their teeth, firing rapidly; the onslaught was terrible, but the charge was met by the jayhawkers with a bold front and steady aim. The guerrillas were beaten back and divided. Cole Younger, with a handful of desperate fighters, was singled out, and the enemy literally rode him down, wounding him and every one of his men. John McDowell was struck hard in the shoulder and his horse shot from under him, holding his foot between the saddle and ground. He called to Younger for help, and his cry was not in vain, for, though it seemed that certain death followed a return. Younger called on Todd to charge, and through the driving hail of bullets, Cole rushed back, bleeding as he was, from a flesh wound in the arm, and released his comrade, lifting him into the saddle and mounting behind. The fight continued furiously for about twenty minutes, when the jayhawkers, though holding their own, were reinforced by another detachment, and then Younger and Todd were driven precipitately across the prairie and into the woods, when superior riding enabled them to escape, but not without serious loss.

The guerrillas returned to Missouri, and at the crossing of Big Blue, where the charred timbers of the old bridge gave evidence of Quantrill's visit and line of retreat, they caught six militiamen and made quick work of them; after shooting their bodies full of bullets, a large pole was cut and stretched across the road, resting in the forks of a tree on each side. The dead militiamen were then hung to the pole, their bodies dangling over the road, as a warning that the guerrillas were on active duty again in Jackson county.

# COLE YOUNGER'S ESCAPE THROUGH THE STRATEGY OF A NEGRO WOMAN.

His first wound giving him some trouble. Cole Younger determined to visit his mother, who needed the comfort of her son in the new sorrow which had just fallen so heavily upon her in the loss of her daughters. Accordingly, he left his men in charge of Todd and, unaccompanied, rode into Cass county, reaching his home, under the cover of night, on the 13th of January. Notwithstanding the secrecy with which he made the visit, there were so many spies on his track, that, scarcely had he entered the house, before his presence became known to the militia stationed at Harrisonville. One hundred men quickly surrounded the house and, conducting their movements with much caution, they were climbing the fence before their approach was suspected. Cole was in a trap, and through his brain coursed the events of a life, forced by what he believed was impending death. Hope for once had entirely forsaken him, and he thought of nothing save his pistols, which he might empty in the face of his executioners before his arm became paralyzed by a fatal bullet. Living with the Younger family was an aged colored woman, who had been a second mother to all the children and whose love for Cole was as warm as ever mother gave her child. With the intuition of a woman in moments of great peril, the old aunty became equal to the emergency, and, with the celerity of youth, she gathered a bed-quilt and flung it about her, concealing Cole beneath it and her ample crinoline. A loud knock at the door brought a response from the old colored woman who, in an unexcited tone of voice, and with confidence in her ability to perform her strategy successfully, asked what was wanted. "Open the door and we will tell you," came a voice from the outside.

Without manifesting any trepidation, old aunty opened wide the door, to admit the heavily armed and prepared men, a dozen of them. The night was dark and cold, but the honest face of that aged colored savior, in the light which shone from the little lamp on the table, gave no appearance of cunning or suspicion. Cole's thoughts, however, were burning his very brain, as he crouched under the convoluted protection of the old negress' skirts and blanket.

"Where is Cole Younger? We know he is in the house, and it would save us time and yourselves trouble, if he would deliver himself up to us," said the lieutenant in charge of the men now in the house.

Edging herself up between two chairs, the old colored mother, by proxy, responded: "Bress de Lawd, honeys. Mars' Cole haint been in dis house fer mor'n six months; and is it him you want?" and the old negro laughed heartily. "Well, you am de warst mistaken men dis side ob Gilhead. Mars' Cole here! why, dat does beat de Jews ob Jerusalem; now, if you can't beleebe dis old nigger jes look de house ober an ef you fines him you can take de wool offin my head."

Notwithstanding the earnest words of aunty the Federals made a search, and while they were lifting the feather beds and peering into closets, the old negro remarked: "Well, I'll jes step on de outside and see who's aroun'." Suspicion never attaching to the jolly old black soul, she was enabled to make her deception thorough, and though her appearance was rather bulky about the extremities, darkness did not reveal it. Moving in a straddling gait, which would have been certain to suggest an investigation had it been day, the aunty and her charge reached the outbuildings, she talking all the time as if anxious to engage some of the Federals in conversation, but in reality to locate the outer line of the guards. It was a clear passage now, and when they reached a place of safety, Cole arose from his cramped position and actually kissed his colored deliverer, but he had done that a thousand times before, a habit acquired in infancy. His horse was hitched back of the orchard, two hundred yards from the house, and fortunately the Federals had not found it. Mounting quickly Cole rode away in the darkness for the old haunts in Sny hills, which he reached without further adventure.

# CHRISTMAS FROLIC IN KANSAS CITY.

Christmas was coming on apace, and as it was impossible for the guerrillas to celebrate it while surrounded by thousands of Federals, Cole Younger decided to commemorate the day by revenging his father's death. Although it was never absolutely known who composed the party who so cruelly assassinated Col. Henry Younger, yet Cole was always satisfied that certain persons whom he knew had some connection with that crime. Among those thus suspected was a young lieutenant named Walley, whom Cole hated with a prejudice blind as revenge. They had been enemies, in fact, since boyhood; dividing their feelings over the smiles of a school girl whose childish favors were reserved for Cole.

Kansas City was in the hands of the Federals, twenty-five hundred strong, and every road leading thence was picketed so strongly that cunning and extraordinary bravery could alone pierce the lines.

Through friendly sources Cole Younger learned that Walley and his company were in Kansas City, and would spend the holidays enjoying the good things of the place. He immediately formed a plan to reach that city and glut his vengeance on all he could find whom he had believed participated in the assassination of his father. Accordingly he communicated with Todd, Taylor, Cunningham, Traber and Clayton, of his command, and acquainted each with his daring scheme. Each man signified his willingness to follow Cole and execute his orders.

On the 23d of December, the six guerrillas clothed themselves in Federal cavalry uniforms and set out for Kansas City. They had no difficulty in passing the pickets, as squads were continually coming in without the countersign. When they reached the town, which was after dark on Christmas eve, they dismounted in the south-east part of the town and left their horses in charge of Zach Traber. The five then made an examination of all the haunts of the place with the hope of locating Walley or his command.

The crowded condition of the saloons, and revelry in the fast houses near the levee, gave the guerrillas an excellent opportunity to discover the place of their victims. On the south side of the public square there were a number of low dives and gambling dens, which Cole and his men did not visit until nearly midnight. They entered one of the saloons which occupied a central position in the block, and no sooner had Todd's eyes taken an inventory of the occupants, than he whispered: "Cole, here are six of the fellows you have been looking for so anxiously."

"So they are," responded Cole, "I should like the privilege of killing them all myself."

"Be quiet," said Todd, "and let me arrange this little Christmas frolic; you shall have your revenge."

The guerrillas walked in, laughing, and strode up to the bar. "Come up, gentlemen, and have something with us," said Todd.

The six Federals were engaged in playing seven-up, three being at two different tables. They were all perceptibly under the influence of liquor, and in a condition to speedily accept Todd's invitation. After drinking, the Federals resumed their games, and the guerrillas went over into a corner of the saloon by themselves, to agree upon the plan of execution. Seated together, Todd was the first to speak: "We want to do this job scientifically and cause as little excitement as possible. There are six of them and only five of us, so we will accord you the honor, Cole, of killing two. Let the signal be: First, 'Let's have a drink.' When this is said, we will each move up behind our victims with pistols under the capes of our coats. The second word will be; 'Who said drink?' at this every man shall draw and fire, and see to it that we have no misses."

"That is good," responded Cole, "and it shall be carried out to the letter. The point of the whole thing, however, is how to get out and avoid arrest I think I can plan that satisfactorily. The moment our pistols are discharged we will move out of the saloon together and, without hurry, separate and mix with the crowd on Main street. Each man will then use his own judgment in reaching Traber and the horses, but every one will be expected to meet there within fifteen or twenty minutes after we leave here."

Everything was now fixed for the terrible deed.

"Let's have a drink!" said Cole Younger.

At this the five guerrillas arose and walked toward the six doomed Federals; the latter merely looked around to see if the invitation extended to them, but nothing further being spoken, they resumed the game.

"Who said drink?" came from the lips of Todd, and at the same instant there was a crack of pistols, only one shot being fired out of time, and the deed was accomplished. Six souls launched so suddenly into eternity! It was a game with Death in which the cunning old reaper held all the trumps.

The moment the shots were fired, the bar-keeper raised the alarm, but the guerrillas stepped leisurely onto the sidewalk, and from those they met running to the scene the murderers eagerly inquired the cause of so much excitement. The city was soon in arms; every soldier was called into line, the patrols sent out in trebled force, and hurried orders were issued to arrest every man found on the streets.

The guerrillas made their way separately, but rapidly, to the spot where Traber was holding their horses, and mounting, they rode swiftly out upon the Independence highway. To every command "halt," they replied with their pistols and, though pursued and shot at, every one of the guerrillas reached a place of safety without having received a scratch.

# MRS. YOUNGER FORCED TO FIRE HER OWN HOME.

The wild fever of war, in its desperate rage, caused the perpetration of such horrors, that a reference to them makes the heart grow sick. But in all the intense agony suffered by so many thousands, whose ill fortunes threw them across the pathway of that demon of slaughter, none were more bitterly visited with sorrow, than Mrs. Younger, and the hand of affliction, which was laid upon her, was never raised until it banked the earth over her grave.

In the early part of the great sectional conflict, her devoted husband was sacrificed upon the altar of desperate passion and remorseless greed. The main support of the stricken family she then saw leave the desolated roof and creep out into a very wilderness of devastation, where, instead of the sweet cry of song-birds, there was the shrill whistle of death, and the soughing trees became funeral dirges. But these were but initiatory sorrows, preparing the way for advanced degrees of intensified distress. She was doomed to receive the mangled forms of three loving daughters, their fair faces and bodies torn to death by the falling timbers of their demolished prison. Still her afflictions grew on apace. A brutal soldiery learned what she had given up in the mad fury of war, and then they added persecutions to her other griefs. The boys left to comfort her, were hunted, although they had committed no crime; John was hung and James chased at the point of the merciless bayonet into the fastnesses of the bluffs; her harvests were confiscated and at last she was forced to flee into Cass county, with the accumulations of honest labor dissipated like the winds. But she found no rest in her new abode; the brutal instincts of her persecutors followed her like a hound, snuffing blood, pursues the wounded deer. Here, in a little home, without either the power or disposition to avenge the cruelties she had so long suffered, a party of twenty-two Federals appeared suddenly, on the 9th of February, 1863, and commanded her to tell the hiding-place of her son Coleman; she did not know, and had she known, what mother would have betrayed her own boy? Threats accomplishing nothing, this brave squad, with cocked and pointed carbines, compelled Mrs. Younger to set fire to her own house and she was then held a captive until the last timber was consumed. There was a deep snow on the ground at the time, and through this the poor woman trudged three miles to a neighbor's house for shelter.

Some time after the burning of her house, Mrs. Younger removed to the home of her brother-in-law, Lycurgas Jones, in Clay county.

Stung to desperation by such persecutions, James Younger, though only fifteen years of age, joined Quantrill, with the hope of being able to avenge his mother's wrongs. But this only resulted in additional sorrow, for, in the following year, James was captured at the fight in Kentucky, where Quantrill met his death, and was confined in the military prison at Alton, Illinois, until June, 1866.

The exposure and dreadful suffering Mrs. Younger had endured for more than two years completely wrecked her health, and she fell a prey to that insidious monster, consumption. Cole went to Texas, after the war, for the purpose of preparing his mother another home, but she was too feeble for removal, and the closing scene of her latterly wretched life occurred on the 10th of May, 1870.

# A BITTER WINTER AND PERSISTENT SKIRMISHING.

The winter of 1862-3 will exist in chronology as one of the most bitterly cold periods of history. Everything was literally frozen up, and north of the Mason and Dixon line the militia lay in enforced inactivity. Cole Younger, with forty of his men, hibernated in the Sny hills with "dug outs" for protection. These buildings consisted of an excavation in the ground, covered with ridge-pole and brush supporting a layer of earth. Here the month of January was spent, predatory incursions being made every few days for forage and provisions; but in February the weather moderated to such an extent as permitted the guerrillas to resume operations. Quantrill visited Richmond and applied for a commission, which the Confederate Secretary of War refused on account of the reputation the renowned guerrilla had acquired by his merciless warfare. Upon his return to camp offensive measures were renewed.

On the 8th of February, Cole Younger and his command fell on thirty Federal cavalrymen under Lieutenant Jefferson, three miles west of Pleasant Hill. The fight was a terrible one, notwithstanding the superior force of the guerrillas. Younger led the attack and struck the Federals furiously, but Jefferson proved a hero and stemmed the onslaught so bravely that the guerrillas were checked, but only for a moment, when Bill Hulse, one of the best carbine shots in the service, shot the heroic lieutenant and the impetuous charge which followed swooped up and swept out into eternity all but four of the Federals, who escaped by superior horsemanship. The guerrillas' loss was only five men.

It was this year, 1863, which gave to the war Bill Anderson, a name clustering with terrors like Medusa's head, and Frank and Jesse James threw off their youth and leaped into the dreadful vortex of battle and slaughter.

Long fighting with no source from whence to recruit, gradually reduced the guerrillas, and their policy was changed from attacking superior forces to waylaying squads, shooting pickets, capturing mail couriers, and harassing the enemy without exposing themselves. The unmerciful, inhuman cruelties perpetrated by the guerrillas during this year can never be measured. Anderson taught his men that mercy was unmanly, that compassion was a crime in the eyes of heaven. Meeting non-combatants, couriers, or furloughed militia, it was an inflexible rule to kill them; every cross-path had its victim, and the highways were fairly drunk with blood.

Near Westport, in the latter part of June, Jarrette and Gregg, with ten men, approached an old-time country tavern kept by a good-natured old man named Hudson. It was after dark, and Gregg was the one to raise the landlord.

"Hello!" shouted the stern guerrilla.

Old man Hudson got up and appeared at the door in his night-gown. "Hello!" responded the landlord.

"We want to stay all night, old man, and being very tired and hungry we would like some supper," spoke Gregg,

"Well, gentlemen," replied Mr. Hudson, "I can have some supper set for you, but I am very sorry to say that every bed in my house is occupied, and even the barn loft is full."

At this the guerrillas passed around the house and soon found that the old man was entertaining a dozen Federal cavalrymen. Proceeding cautiously, four of them climbed up into the stable loft and there found three sleeping Federals. It was the work of a moment to cut their throats and consummate the dreadful deed before an alarm was given. The guerrillas then went to the house, and being admitted, they seized old man Hudson and cut his throat, after which they found their victims sleeping soundly, and like cattle led to the slaughter every Federal in the house was mercilessly murdered and left in that dreamless sleep, flooded with their own blood. What a direful sight, and what anguish was that which fell upon the family of that hospitable old man! Alone in their solitary habitation with none for company save the now bloodless corpses of father, husband and twelve clothed in the uniforms which proved their funeral cerements. Added to this the torch was applied with the double hope of hiding the crime and destroying that whereby the others left of that household lived. It is proper to state here, however, that Cole Younger had no connection whatever with this infamous outrage, and that he condemned the perpetrators as violently as human being could.

Following fast upon this massacre came many others. Bill Anderson, the prairie vulture, was in the saddle and killing defenceless men everywhere. He neither asked for quarter nor gave any; his mission was to slay and spare not. No ropes were required, the pistol was quicker, or the knife more certain. Near Olathe Anderson struck a squad of infantry, and by surprising them put to death every one. Two days afterward he came upon twelve men driving wagons loaded with corn; they were not told to pray, nor would time have been given had they asked it; twelve men tumbled off their wagons and fell in the roadway with pistol balls in their head. The corn and wagons were burned and the horses appropriated.

But the killing was not all on the side of the guerrillas; the Federals adopted a similar mode of warfare and the policy was to kill man for man. Philip Bucher was shot at his home in Westport by order of Maj. Ransom, the wife of the doomed man clinging to his neck begging for his life. Henry Rout was hung in plain view of his house; and then the shooting and hanging continued without the straining of mercy even by either side.

The execution of men, and women too, had become so common that both sides seemed to vie with each other in the demonstration of their brutal instincts. It was this unmerciful warfare which led at last to the holocaust at Lawrence. More than three hundred men had been gathered together by Quantrill for the express purpose of desolating that town and capturing the vast wealth known to be accumulated there. That the acquisition of this treasure was the prime object of the attack, was frankly admitted to the writer by one of the chief participants in that matchless raid.

It was on the 21st of August, 1863, that the chief of evil, Quantrill, descended upon that peaceful Kansas town, and with pistol, sword and torch massacred the defenceless inhabitants, plundered homes, banks and stores, filled the streets with blood, and then to complete the desolation applied the fire brands until the streets blended with the buildings in one vast block of lurid flames. The very soul grows sick at the contemplation of such infamies, such crimes as pollute the very name of humanity, and make us almost wish we were not men, to have to bear the odium which such dreadful deeds imposes on our race.

After the terrible work was completed, Quantrill, gathering all the money and valuables he could secure, turned his face again towards Missouri; but the return march was accompanied by hardships scarcely anticipated; the militia swarmed on his trail and struck him right and left; his columns were broken and scattered; not a moment for rest was permitted, and he gained Missouri only by separating and letting each man look to his own safety. Many of the guerrillas never returned to their homes again, for in the continued retreat and fighting, more than a score were left dead on the prairies. When the guerrillas left Lawrence, they carried with them money and valuables estimated at $3,000,000; this is the sum fixed by George

Shepherd, but they reached Missouri with less than one-half that amount, the balance being lost, in the retreat, out of saddle bags, sacks, etc., in which the treasure was carried, and on the persons of those killed.

After Lawrence came the famous order of Gen. Ewing, requiring all the men in Bates, Vernon and Cass counties to abandon their property and report at once to the nearest military headquarters for service. The force of Federals increased rapidly through the instrumentality of this order, and Quantrill found himself in desperate quarters, day and night. The warfare became even more cruel than before; revenge was not satisfied by the mere killing, but extended frequently to the mutilation of the victims. Squads were massacred almost daily, and life went for naught wherever found.

The days of the guerrillas were numbering fast; one by one they were shot out of the ranks, and gradually Quantrill felt the Federals, like the folds of the constrictor, gathering around him with more certain grip to crush his life out. On the 10th of September, three weeks after Lawrence, the now straggling band was called together, and being clothed in the uniform of Federals, marched away from the old haunts to the South. On that march Quantrill had a brush at Baxter Springs, and drew off on account of superior forces; but, on the following day, he met Gen. Blunt with two hundred men, and being disguised, the guerrillas had an advantage which they made the most of, riding upon the unsuspecting Federals and putting them to rout with severe loss.

Lieutenant Cole Younger reported to Gen. E. Kirby Smith and, with a company of fifty men, went into quarters at Bastrop, Louisiana. In the spring of 1864, he co-operated with a large force and did effective service for the Confederates in attacking small convoys and capturing supply trains.

In the early part of 1865, Cole Younger was commissioned by the Confederate Secretary of War, to recruit a regiment in California. He took a small squad of men with him and on the route encountered some bands of Apache Indians, with whom he had several severe fights, losing half his men. When Lee surrendered, Cole was at Los Angeles and, taking that act as a final culmination of the war, he remained in California for several months, and then returned to Texas.

James Younger joined the guerrillas in 1864, and was one of the command under Lieutenant George Shepherd. He was a brave soldier, and like Cole, preserved his honor by ever refusing to ill-treat a prisoner or commit a wrong on a woman; both boys defended and assisted Temales, regardless of circumstances, and their generosity and mercy is gratefully remembered by hundreds to-day, whose lives were spared and property saved, by the intercession of the Youngers.

The history and remarkable adventures of the Younger Brothers since the war, will be found narrated in chronological order in the succeeding chapters.

# PROGRESS OF CRIMES WHICH THE WAR INAUGURATED.

The evils begotten by intestine wars, like those of a seductive habit, increase by gradual insinuation until normal human nature is masked by a decision of character, whose prominent propensity is always evil. The bivouac on the field, the ambuscade, and the battle, with all its horrors of soul-sickening carnage, do not represent the product of these multiplied scourges of human life; they are often but the prelude to more desperate tragedies. The most sentimental heart becomes calloused by contact with cruelties, and in the mellow days of innocence, the eye that would veil itself with the tears of compassion at the slightest object of suffering, may become so familiarized with the sight of crime, that at last, with clear and steel-cold vision, it springs to the aid of the hand that plunges a fatal dagger through the most guiltless heart. This is one of the consequences of civil war. When the great armies of the two estranged sections folded away their tents, replaced their weapons in the armories of the nation, and returned to the maize fields, that had grown tangled with the briers and growth which neglect cultivates, there were those in whose ears the tocsin of war echoed, like fresh peals, and those refused to abandon an occupation of pillage and destruction, made congenial by long pursuit. It was the guerrilla and jayhawker during the great conflict, who created new fields of operations, and carved a highway to the scenes of fatal greed and bitter vengeance. Among this class, over whose head no longer floated a banner as an emblem of their principles, were the Younger Brothers. John and James had not reached a mature age, when the antipodal war closed its horrors and was hidden away under the sweet canopy of peace, but they had matured the wayward hopes of border heroism, and when the new time, or aftermath of unlawful cruelties, was at hand, they joined their fortunes with those over whose persons there was no protecting panoply, and boldly took the step which, soon after, made them hunted outlaws.

# THE TERRIBLE "BLACK OATH."

In the early organizations of the guerrillas, Quantrill, whose shrewdness and military tact, find few parallels in history, adopted a measure which, though terrible in some of its aspects, was like a salvation clause in his desperate warfare, and saved him and his band from extermination more than a hundred times. Quantrill would have been a Union man, so some of his comrades declare, but for the murder of his brother and almost fatal wounding of himself by a company of jayhawkers, in 1856, as he was traveling overland through Kansas for California. After Quantrill recovered from his deep and dreadful wounds, thenceforth he sought for nothing except revenge; his life he never cast up in the reckoning of his adventure, and extremities he cared nothing for. When men were enlisted under his command, by a magnetic power for dissipating fear and heroizing the lovers of unmerciful warfare, he taught them how to play with dead men, and crave the most daring and hazardous undertakings. As a capsheaf of his instructions he invented the "Black Oath," black being the color he admired, because it suggested danger and death. It was never administered except after night, when the stars were faded and the sky hung heavy with ominous clouds; or, when nature refused to lend her stygian curtain to such a drama, those qualified to administer the obligation repaired to the deepest shades, with the candidates, and there imposed the ceremonies. The oath was as follows:

"The purpose of war is to kill! God himself has made it honorable, in the defence of principles, for did he not cast Lucifer out of heaven, and relegate rebellious angels to the shades of hell! The love of life cannot be measured, under two conditions: one is, when our surroundings are happy and our attachments numerous; the other is, when our liberties are subjugated, peace destroyed, and everything we hold most dear torn from us, until we realize that contentment, love, hope, have forever vanished. We fight that the former condition may be regained, and we fight, because the latter leaves us no other occupation.

"You have voluntarily signified a desire to cast your fortunes with us; by so doing remember that our purpose is to tear down, lay waste, despoil and kill our enemies; mercy belongs to sycophants and emasculated soldiers, it is no part of a fighter's outfit; to us it is but a vision repugnant to our obligations and our practices. We recognize but one power to separate us in the hour of peril, and to succor one another at all hazards, we have pledged ourselves more sacredly, and are bound by ties much stronger than honor can impose. With this understanding of what will be required of you, are you willing to proceed? [The candidate assenting, the following oath is administered, being repeated by the candidate as the initiatory officer speaks it slowly by broken sentences:]

"In the name of God and Devil, the one to punish and the other to reward, and by the powers of light and darkness, good and evil, here, under the black arch of heaven's avenging symbol, I pledge and consecrate my heart, my brain, my body, and my limbs, and swear by all the powers of hell and heaven to devote my life to obedience to my superiors; that no danger or peril shall deter me from executing their orders; that I will exert every possible means in my power for the extermination of Federals, jayhawkers, and their abettors; that in fighting those whose serpent trail has winnowed the fair fields and possessions of our allies and sympathizers, I will show no mercy, but strike, with an avenging arm, so long as breath remains.

"I further pledge my heart, my brain, my body, and my limbs, never to betray a comrade; that I will submit to all the tortures cunning mankind can inflict, and suffer the most horrible death, rather than reveal a single secret of this organization, or a single word of this, my oath.

"I further pledge my heart, my brain, my body, and my limbs, never to forsake a comrade when there is hope, even at the risk of great peril, of saving him from falling into the hands of our enemies; that I will sustain Quantrill's guerrillas with my might and defend them with my blood, and, if need be, die with them; in every extremity I will never withhold my aid, nor abandon the cause with which I now cast my fortunes, my honor and my life. Before violating a single clause or implied pledge of this obligation, I will pray to an avenging God and an unmerciful devil to tear out my heart and roast it over flames of sulphur; that my head may be split open and my brains scattered over the earth; that my body may be ripped up and my bowels torn out and fed to carrion birds; that each of my limbs may be broken with stones, and then cut off, by inches, that they may feed the foulest birds of the air; and lastly, may my soul be given unto torment, that it may be submerged in melted metal and be stifled by the fumes of hell, and may this punishment be meeted out to me through all eternity, in the name of God and devil, Amen."

At the conclusion of the oath, the candidate was turned successively to the east, west, north and south, while four men, clothed in red and black suits, and wearing hideous masks, representing the devil, drew their long, keen swords and presented them at the newly-made guerrilla, one pointing at his heart, another at the head, another at the abdomen and the other shifting his weapon from the arms and feet.

This completed the ceremony and thenceforth the accepted comrade went forth on his mission of massacre.

# THE FIRST BANK ROBBERY — AT LIBERTY, MISSOURI.

The war had made the guerrillas expert in massacring repugnant citizens, and in appropriating the property of their victims. Many of the old crowd were banded together by the sinews of the "black oath," and scarcely had the smoke of battle been lifted up and assimilated with the refreshing dew clouds of heaven before plans were matured for the robbing of country banks.

On the 20th of January, 1866, the sheriff of Harrison county attempted to execute a capias for the arrest of Bill Reynolds, in Pleasant Hill, who was under indictment for crimes committed during the war. Geo. Maddox and N. P. Hayes were in town at the time, and as the three were members of the same organization, resistance to the officer was made. It became necessary for the sheriff to summon a posse of citizens to his assistance. A fight in the open street then ensued, ending in the death of Reynolds and Hayes and the capture of Maddox. Threats of an attack on the town by guerrillas were rumored, and for several days nearly every male citizen was bearing arms in anticipation of an attempt being made to liberate Maddox.

The excitement was unabated in Pleasant Hill until the 14th of February, when the robbery of the Clay County Savings Association at Liberty, Missouri, was reported. The reason why rumors were so persistently circulated of an intended attempt to deliver Maddox, was now clearly understood to be for the purpose of making the surprise on Liberty more complete. Early in the morning of St. Valentine's day, a squad of the old guerrillas, numbering an even dozen, rode into Liberty from different directions and meeting in the public square they disposed themselves as follows: three of the robbers were stationed some distance from the bank at eligible positions, which would most readily detect any centralizing attack or suspicious movement of the citizens; the other nine rode directly up to the front of the bank, where two of the number dismounted and entered with drawn revolvers. The hour being early, luckily for the bandits there was no one in the bank except the cashier, Mr. Bird, and his son. A pistol was presented at the head of each, and under threats of instant death in case of refusal, Mr. Bird opened the bank vault from which the sum of seventy-two thousand dollars was taken and crammed into a pair of saddle bags carried for the purpose. As the robbers were regaining their horses for flight, Mr. Bird thrust his head out of a window and called to a little boy by the name of Wymore, whom he saw passing, telling him that a robbery had been committed and to raise the alarm. As the little fellow, not more than twelve years of age, raised the cry of "robbers! help!" he was fired on by the bandits and fell dead with five fatal bullets in his body. The robbers then began firing indiscriminately and yelling with savage fury, so that for some time after the bandits had departed the citizens were too badly intimidated to think of pursuit. A posse, under the leadership of the sheriff, was organized about one hour afterward, however, and started out on a spirited chase. The trail led to Mount Gilead Church, where the evidence of bank-paper showed that the robbers had tarried a few moments to divide the spoils. It was also evident that the band had separated and taken various directions so as to elude pursuit, which they accomplished so effectively that not one of the bandits was apprehended. Jim White and J. F. Edmunson were arrested in St. Joseph a short time afterward on suspicion, and a warrant was issued for Bill Chiles, their partner, but he escaped. The preliminary examination failed to disclose any evidence showing their complicity in the robbery, and they were promptly released, though to this day there are hundreds of good citizens who feel that Edmunson, Chiles and White were members of the gang. Among the bandits, positively recognized as participants in the robbery, were Oil Shepherd, Red Honkers and Bud Pence, but they eluded the officers cleverly, and very soon the chase was abandoned. The excitement subsided and the event was partially forgotten by the citizens, nearly all of whom were afraid to manifest any particular anxiety to bring the robbers to justice, because assassinations on the highway, and even by the fireside, had become too familiar.

The majority of Clay county residents believe that Cole Younger and the James Boys were the ones who conceived the robbery, and that it was under their orders it was perpetrated. It would be transgressing the duties of the writer, because prejudice would be manifest, to unhesitatingly declare that the Younger Boys are responsible for the robbery. The trail is given and the reader left to draw his own conclusions, understanding that these outlaws deny any and all knowledge of the persons who committed the robbery.

The sack of the Liberty bank was the first of the second series of guerrilla crimes, and being accomplished with such perfect success, and the collection of a booty so considerable inspired many other similar surprises which will be related in their regular order.

# JOHN YOUNGER'S FIRST FIGHT.

There never was a Younger, perhaps, who did not possess great courage, and this spirit was manifested in each of the boys at a remarkably early age. The brothers all matured rapidly, however, and in the years of adolescence, they were considered men because of their size. In January, 1866, Cole Younger, while remaining near the scenes of his childhood, but yet ostracised, because of the part he took during the furious years of 61-65, had occasion to send his pistol to Independence for repairs, as the dog-spring was broken. John Younger, his brother, who was then only fourteen years of age, hitched up a team and drove to Independence, taking the pistol with him. The weapon was loaded, and in repairing it, the gun-smith allowed the loads to remain. Some time in the afternoon of the day in question, the exact date being forgotten, John got the pistol, paid for the repairs, and then walked up the street fronting the public square, where he entered a store, which already contained about a dozen country people. Among the number was an Irishman, named Gillcreos, who had only recently been released from jail, where he was confined for some offence. Gillcreos had been a Union soldier, and was nearly always boasting of his soldier record. During the general conversation John Younger's name was called, and when Gillcreos learned that the boy before him was a veritable brother of Cole Younger, he at once opened his batteries of abuse. John acted as though completely frightened, returning no answer to the epithets flung at him by the Irishman, and using every means to avoid a difficulty. Finding John so passive to insults, Gillcreos at length, without the slightest provocation, administered a severe kick to the peaceable boy. This was too much to bear. John showed the temper that was slumbering by saying: "If you do that again I'll kill you." Gillcreos immediately kicked John again, much harder than before. In an instant the pistol was out and fired, the ball striking the insulting Irishman directly in the heart and killing him, without a groan proceeding from the victim's lips.

After the shooting, John ran out of the store and, reaching his team, he quickly cut the lead-horse loose and mounting, rode away. On the following day, however, he was captured and taken back to Independence.

Upon examining Gillcreos, after his death, a large stung-shot was found on his wrist, and it was conclusively proven, at the preliminary trial, that the victim, laboring under great excitement without proper cause, manifested a determination to kill John Younger, and would, undoubtedly, have killed the boy, had John failed to fire at the moment he did.

The proof of justification was so overwhelming, that the youth was exonerated by the coroner's jury, and the grand jury refused to review the evidence, considering the original verdict eminently just.

# DESPERATE ATTEMPT AT JAIL DELIVERY.

Joab Perry, an ex-guerrilla and notorious law-breaker, was arrested on the 10th of June and lodged in the jail at Independence. His character and associations were such that an attempt at delivery was anticipated, and a strong guard was maintained about the jail. On the 14th, succeeding, five well-armed and mounted men rode into the town and proceeded directly to the jail, on which they made a desperate attack, and at the second fire the jailer was killed, while the bullet marks on the doors and windows about the jail, bore evidence of the skilful marksmanship of the attacking party. After firing about twenty shots, all of which were ineffectual, save the fatal bullet which killed the jailer, the party wheeled their horses and rode swiftly out of town, having failed in this purpose to liberate their companion. The names of the five men were never given to the public, for the reason that every man in that section knew the desperate character of the Younger and James boys and their comrades; to have manifested any officious interference with these men was to invite their vengeance. It was this reason which prevented active measures, looking to the apprehension of the guerrilla, now outlaw band.

# THE LEXINGTON BANK ROBBERY.

At high noon, on the 30th of October, 1866, five determined men visited Lexington, Missouri, and leisurely hitched their horses in an alley near the banking-house of Alexander Mitchell & Co. Two of the men walked into the bank, meeting the cashier, J. L. Thomas, in the door-way, who went behind the counter, to attend to the wants of the strangers. One of the men handed a $50 7-30 bond to the cashier with the request to have it changed. As Mr. Thomas opened the cash drawer, two more of the robbers appeared at the door with drawn revolvers, the fifth man being left in charge of the horses. It was quick work now, for looking into the muzzles of four deadly pistols, the cashier was compelled to hand over all the money in the bank, $2,000, which being placed in a sack, the robbers coolly walked out of the bank with a parting admonition to Mr. Thomas, that, if he raised any outcry, they would kill him. Mounting their horses, the robbers rode swiftly away, and it was more than an hour after the robbery before a pursuing party was organized. Twelve well-armed citizens started after the bandits and spent two days in a fruitless search for the despoilers. People began to consider the insecurity of country banks and the means for apprehending the daring outlaws; meetings were held and various plans discussed, but in two weeks' time the outrage was almost forgotten.

# THE BANK ROBBERY AT SAVANNAH, MO.

Six months had expired after the Lexington robbery, before another attempt was made to crack a bank and outrage the citizens of a village. The scars produced by the battles on the border were healing, and over the deepest wounds was forming a cicatrix of forgetfulness.

Savannah is the capital seat of Andrew county, a thrifty little place, of twelve or fifteen hundred inhabitants, that had suffered but little from the blight of war. The place contained a small banking institution, under the proprietorship of Judge McLain, with small capital.

On the 2nd of March, 1867, five ex-guerrillas, J. F. Edmunson, Jim White, Bill Chiles, Bud McDaniels, and a fellow named Pope, rode into Savannah in such a manner as indicated they were on important business. It was nearly high noon, and no one was in the bank except the Judge and his son. The bandits rode up and four of them dismounted, leaving their horses in charge of the fifth man. As the four entered the bank with drawn pistols, the Judge looked earnestly over his spectacles, and at once comprehended the character of his customers. He slammed the door of the safe shut, and seizing a revolver, which lay on the bank counter, he met the bandits half-way, but his shots proved ineffectual, while a big navy pistol ball went tearing through his breast which made him sink to the floor as one death-stricken. Young McLain ran into the street and gave the alarm, which brought many citizens to the rescue. The robber left in charge of the horses shouted for the return of his companions, who finding their position becoming very serious, mounted the ready horses and fled.

A posse of twenty-five citizens went in pursuit of the bandits, a few minutes after their hasty departure, and trailed them for a great distance. In the extreme north-west part of Missouri, the citizen squad definitely located Chiles and White, but the indications were also too apparent that others of the band were in the same neighborhood, so that the posse did not have courage sufficient to attempt the capture. Pope and McDaniels were arrested near St. Joseph, Mo., on the 18th of March, but they were both so well fortified with witnesses, who swore an alibi, and thus their release was accomplished, but despite the alibi, there were conclusive circumstances disclosed which left scarcely a possibility of doubt that they were members of the gang, and were accomplices in the attempted bank robbery at Savannah. Judge McLain's wound, though a desperate one, fortunately did not prove fatal, and, after several weeks' suffering and close confinement, he was enabled to resume his duties.

# THE ROBBERY AND BITTER FIGHT AT RICHMOND, MISSOURI.

Comparative little excitement having been occasioned by the futile attempt to rob the Savannah bank, and finding their funds low, a plan was formed for the pillage of the bank at Richmond, Missouri. Accordingly, on the 23d of May a band of outlaws numbering fourteen men, made a descent on the place, headed by Peyton Jones, a well known guerrilla during the war. They charged the place, shouting and firing their pistols at every person they could see. Six of the number, under the sheltering arms of their comrades, forced an entrance into the private bank of Hughes & Mason, from which they secured the sum of four thousand dollars. Mayor Shaw, a brave and efficient officer, seized a pistol and ran across the street where he hoped to concentrate a posse of citizens and give battle to the outlaws. The moment he was discovered, three of the bandits rode swiftly upon him, and though the brave mayor fired with what aim he could command, it was too imperfect, however, for execution, and he fell fighting in the street, with four bullets in his body.

The robbers next began an attack upon the jail, which at that time held a number of prisoners whose arrest, it was claimed, was due to the expression of secession sentiment. The jailer, B. G. Griffin, and his son fifteen years of age, were at the jail, and they received their assailants with remarkable bravery. The boy stationed himself behind a tree and was emptying a revolver in the face of the outlaws, when he was surrounded and shot to death. Mr. Griffin, seeing the fate of his brave boy, rushed up and standing over the lifeless body fought like the frenzied man he was until, pierced by seven bullets, he fell dead across the bleeding and lifeless body of his son. By this time the citizens recovered their lost nerves, and from a score of windows there poured the rifle and pistol flame, yet throughout the combat not a single robber was harmed.

This more desperate outrage than any previously committed by the banditti, aroused the citizens of Richmond like a tocsin of war. A number of the outlaws had been recognized, and the sheriff and one hundred volunteer deputies determined to capture the gang. Business was entirely suspended for three days, until after the burial of the victims, and the heaviest capitalists in the district subscribed means and lent every possible influence to the effort developed to apprehend the murderous robbers. Warrants were issued for the arrest of Jim and John White, Peyton Jones, Dick Burns, Ike Flannery, Andy McGuire and Allen Palmer. Why the name of the latter was included, it is difficult to tell, because Palmer was at that time in Kansas City working for J. E. Shawhan & Co. Neither the Younger nor James Boys were included in the capias, though that one or more of them were in the fight seems certain from the later testimony of reputable citizens of Richmond.

Kansas City sent out a squad of eighteen men in pursuit of the robbers, and on the 26th, three days after the fight and robbery, they learned that Peyton, or Payne Jones, as he was called, was stopping at the house of Mr. Evans, two miles west of Independence. The squad decided to capture Jones at night, that under cover of darkness they might surround him before discovery. When the shades of dusk appeared, the posse, taking Dr. Noland's little girl along as guide, proceeded cautiously on the highway to Mr. Evans' house. It was raining very hard and the darkness was almost impenetrable. Marshall Mizery, in charge of the squad, disposed his men around the house and was just about giving the word "close up," when Jones, aroused by some means not understood, as the squad had preserved the most perfect quiet, flung open the door and leaped into the yard with a double-barreled shot-gun and two revolvers. The moment he struck the ground Jones discharged both barrels of the gun, killing a young man named B. H. Wilson and fatally wounding Dr. Noland's little daughter. After firing the gun Jones threw it away and made a rush for the woods one hundred yards distant. The extreme darkness and knowledge position of the surrounding men compelled the posse to withhold their fire lest they might kill some of their own number. Pursuit was, however, given, and continued for more than two miles, but the extreme darkness only served to divide the party, and the fifty or more shots they fired might as well have been aimed at the inky clouds overhead. It was afterward claimed that Jones had received a slight wound in the shoulder, but this report was doubtless circulated to create a belief that the expedition had not resulted entirely fruitlessly, especially as they were compelled to return to Kansas City with the dead bodies of two of their own number.

On the night following the attempt to capture Payne Jones, another party, of ten men from Richmond, caught Dick Burns, and without giving him time to pray, with reckless haste they hung him to a large tree in a lonely spot where it was thought the buzzards and crows would pick him before the vigilante's work was discovered, and so it transpired.

Andy McGuire eluded pursuit for several weeks, but his time came at last. He was caught not far from Warrensburg by a small posse who knew him too well to allow any intercession of the law. They only decorated Andy with a new grass rope and hauled him skyward over the branch of a big oak, with the usual manifestation of sympathy.

Although considerable time had elapsed after the attack on Richmond, yet the people did not allow their desire for revenge to cool; they continued the pursuit, and every few days they learned the names of others connected with the daring and desperate outrage — there was hope for capturing the entire band.

Tom Little was chased from cave to cave, over hills, into lonely places, and driven, at last, to take passage on the Fannie Lewis at Jefferson City. When the boat reached the wharf at St. Louis, the chief of police, having been previously notified, grasped Little and kept him in the St. Louis jail for some time, for fear of lynching, if he were returned to Richmond. Afterward he was taken to Warrensburg, where, the citizens still remembering how Little and Bill Greenwood had, during the previous spring, robbed some of the largest stores and defied arrest, they took him from the jail and left his body oscillating from a large tree, as an example to law-breakers.

Jack Hines and Bill Hulse were also suspected of complicity in the Richmond robbery, and they were so persistently haunted, that it became necessary for them to leave the country. So many were now declared connected with the robbery, and the efforts to accomplish their arrest were so determined, that two or three counties became so excited, that it appeared, for a time, that another guerrilla war was to be inaugurated. The bitterest feelings prevailed and wayside assassinations became so frequent as to put every man in jeopardy. This condition of public insecurity continued for many months, and until several of the leading men of the affected counties organized an effort for pacification, and made such appeals to the different elements as produced, at last, the desired effect, and ended a veritable vendetta.

There were many persons, of course, who asserted that Cole Younger was in the robbery, and some even declared that he was in command of the band, but there is every evidence to show that he was in Texas at the time and was neither connected with, nor had any knowledge of the outrage. He was, in fact, preparing a home for his mother, where she might live so far removed from the scenes which burdened her with sorrows, that the memory of those dreadful deeds might not haunt her so vividly.

# THE RUSSELLVILLE BANK ROBBERY.

The excitement in Missouri over the bank robberies and other outrages, known to have been perpetrated by the same organized band of outlaws, kept the officers of country banks in a state of anxious anticipation for a considerable period of time. This fact being realized by the bandits, they concluded to carry their adventures into other fields. Kentucky, therefore, became the objective point, the selection being made because of a residence in that State by some of the outlaws, which familiarized them with many sections, and thus enabled them to strike with better results and with surer chances for escape. Accordingly, the band left Missouri in the early part of 1868, and took up quarters in Nelson county, Kentucky, where a plan was formed to rob the bank at Russellville, the county seat of Logan county. This place is located in a very rich district in the State, and has a population of about three thousand souls; the country around was known thoroughly to George Shepherd, one of the band, who resided near the town at the time and for two or three years before the robbery was committed. The particulars of the bank plundering are graphically given by a correspondent in the Nashville Banner of March 22d, as follows:

"About ten days ago, a man calling himself Colburn, and claiming to be a cattle dealer, offered to sell to Mr. Long a 7-30 note of the denomination of $500. As none of the coupons had been cut off, and the stranger, who pretended to be from Louisville, where the notes were worth a premium, offered it at par and allowed interest, Mr. Long became suspicious and refused to take it. On the 18th he returned again and asked Mr. Long to change him a $100 bill. He was accompanied by a man of forbidding aspect, and suspecting the note to be counterfeit, Mr. Long declined changing it. On the 20th, about 2 P. M., as Mr. Long, Mr. Barclay, clerk in the bank, and Mr. T. H. Simmons, farmer living near Russellville, were sitting behind the counter, Colburn and another man rode up to the door, hitched their horses and entered the bank, three companions remaining outside. They asked for change for a $50 note. Mr. Long pronounced it counterfeit, but was about making a more careful examination, when Colburn drew a revolver, placed its muzzle against his head, and cried out, 'Surrender!' Mr. Long wheeled around and sprang toward the door leading into a room in the rear of the banking office. He hoped thus to make his exit from the building and give the alarm. He was, however, anticipated by one of the robbers, who intercepted him at the door already mentioned, placed a pistol within six or eight inches of his head and fired, without having uttered a word. The ball did no greater injury than grazing Mr. Long's scalp for about two inches, tearing away the hair and flesh, but not fracturing the skull. Mr. L. seized hold of the weapon, and made an effort to wrench it from his assailant, but the robber succeeded in regaining possession of his pistol. He immediately commenced to beat Mr. Long over the head with the butt, and, after a few furiously dealt blows, felled him to the floor. The latter, however, sprang to his feet and again got hold of the pistol, just as the robber was about to cock it for the purpose of giving him the finishing touch. During the scuffle which now took place, Mr. Long managed to reach the back door of the rear room. Here he concentrated his almost exhausted strength into a final effort, freed himself from the clutches of the robber, sprang through the door and closed it after him. He then ran around toward the front part of the building, shouting for assistance. When he reached the street, he found two men sitting on their horses before the entrance to the bank. They were all armed with Spencer's rifles and pistols, and were shooting up and down the street at all citizens who came within range. As Mr. Long ran by, they also fired twelve or fifteen shots at him, but, fortunately, without effect.

"Inside the bank, while Mr. Long was struggling with the fellow above mentioned, and before Messrs. Barclay and Simmons could rise from their seats, the latter were confronted by Colburn and his companion with cocked revolvers and threats of instant death in case the least show of resistance was made. Neither of the gentlemen was armed and they had to accept the situation with the best grace they could command. As soon as Mr. Long made his retreat by the back door, his antagonist returned to the banking office and assisted in the work of plunder. One of the robbers stood guard over Messrs. Barclay and Simmons, while Colburn and the other proceeded to clean out the establishment. They appeared to have an exact knowledge of its resources. As was afterward ascertained, Colburn had made some cautious inquiries as to its capital, deposits, etc., and we have already shown that his previous visits had enabled him to make a thorough inspection of the interior. In the cash drawer they found over nine thousand dollars in currency. From the vault, the door of which was standing open, they took several bags of gold and silver. This specie consisted principally of dollars, half-dollars and quarters, and had been placed in the bank on special deposit by several of the neighboring farmers. The amount has never been ascertained, but it will not, we understand, exceed five thousand dollars. Several private boxes which were on a shelf in the vault and contained bonds were broken open, but none of the bonds were carried off — doubtless because of a fear that they had been registered and would lead to the detection of the robbers. Two robbers kept guard outside while the work of pillaging was going on, and, though the alarm had spread, kept the citizens at bay until a Mr. Owens had the courage to begin firing upon them with a pistol. He was seriously but not dangerously wounded. Finally the sentinels became alarmed and called for their accomplices inside to come out. They quickly complied, bringing with them saddle-bags crammed with gold and greenbacks.

"They were greeted with a heavy volley by a squad of citizens who were advancing up the street. All were soon in their saddles, and, at a signal from Colburn, the party dashed at full speed out of town by the Gallatin pike. Many a leaden missile was sent after them, but beyond the report that one had his arm broken, there is no ground for supposing that any of the shots took effect. Ten minutes later, some forty citizens, mounted on such animals as they could collect from buggies, wagons and hitching posts, started in hot pursuit. All the advantage, except in point of numbers, was with the robbers. They rode splendid horses, and were as completely armed and equipped as the most daring and accomplished highwayman could desire. Five miles from Russellville the trail was lost in the woods, nor was anything heard of Colburn and his men until the 21st, when a dispatch was received here stating that they had crossed the Louisville and Nashville Railroad early in the morning, near Mitchellsville.

"Detective Bligh, of Louisville, was called into the case, and he followed the trail away to the south for seventy-five miles, where it suddenly vanished in Nelson county. One or two of the gang had been recognized by parties on the road, and it took but a very little time to ascertain their associates and friends. Bligh, with another officer named Wm. Gallagher, and some Nelson county people, first raided the house of George Shepherd, who was living in Nelson county. George surrendered after a fight, seeing that he had no chance for escape. He was taken back to Logan county, convicted and served three years. The arrest of George Shepherd had been first made because he was by himself, the others of the gang having been traced to another part of the county. On gathering a posse to capture them, it was found that news of George Shepherd's arrest had gone ahead, and his cousin, Oil Shepherd, had immediately started for Missouri with two or three comrades. Inquiry easily developed information that Jesse James and Cole Younger went with him. It was then satisfactorily shown that Cole must have been the man who called himself Colburn at the bank. It was also found that Jesse James had been "visiting " in Logan county a few weeks before. At that time Jim Younger and Frank James were a hundred times more notorious in Kentucky than Cole and Jesse, because the latter two had not done the State with Quantrill. It was a natural thing then on finding that Jesse and Cole had gone with Shepherd, for the detectives to claim that the other boys were in it too, especially as no trace of a James or Younger could be found anywhere in Nelson county where they had been stopping off and on for a year. So the cry of the 'Jameses and Youngers' was raised. More careful investigation developed the fact that on the day of the robbery, Jesse James was at his hotel in Nelson county. He was slowly recovering from an old wound which would not heal and made it imprudent for him to ride on horseback on any violent trip.

"The romantic version of the raid is that it was undertaken to procure funds to send him on a sea voyage. Frank James had gone to California some months before."

"Bligh followed the retreating raiders till he was satisfied of their destination, and then sent word to the Jackson county, Missouri, authorities to look out for them. Oil Shepherd made a quick trip of it and on arriving, was waited upon by a sheriff's posse. As they summoned him to surrender he broke for the brush and got about twenty bullets, which finished him. The rest of the party were heard from a day or two later and as better information had then been obtained, Bligh and Gallagher went over with requisitions for Cole Younger, Jesse James, John Jarrette and Jim White, who were claimed to be the active assistants of the Shepherds. However, the news of Oil Shepherd's death had given them warning to keep out of the way. The Younger residence was raided, but only the youngsters, John and Bob, were found at home. The balance of the band were never arrested. Bligh still holds that Jesse James was accessory to the job, though he admits he was 75 miles away when it occurred."

There are several facts connected with the Russellville robbery which the correspondence, quoted above, perverts. Colburn, as he rightly suspicions, was Cole Younger, but whatever detective Bligh admits, respecting Jesse

James' absence at the time, it is now positively known that both Jesse and Frank James were active participants in the pillage of that bank.

George Shepherd, while he would not positively state who his accomplices were in the robbery, yet gave the writer some information from which conclusions were readily reached. Instead of being captured at his home in Nelson county, Shepherd states that he was chased nearly seven hundred miles; that he believed pursuit had been abandoned, and upon going into a drug store in a small town in Tennessee, three men jumped upon him suddenly and pinioned his arms before he could make any resistance. Shepherd further told the writer that, before this capture, he had resolved never to be taken alive, but that the peculiar circumstances of his arrest prevented him from carrying out his resolve. During the period of his penitentiary service, Shepherd made his escape and succeeded in getting nearly thirty miles from the prison, but was recaptured and compelled to serve his time.

The Russellville band consisted of Cole and Jim Younger, Jesse and Frank James, and George and Shepherd.

# THE TRAGIC RESULTS OF A HORSE RACE.

After the escape from Russellville the band divided up and Cole Younger went to Bastrop, Louisiana, where, for a time, he was stationed during the war, and had a few acquaintances. He took with him South a blooded horse which, though ill in appearance, had developed extraordinary speed. Cole was a horse racer, and, in fact, he never hesitated to lay a wager on either cards or horses, having a marked penchant for gambling.

While spending a few months in Louisiana among the sporting fraternity, a horse race was proposed; in fact, it was an every Saturday recreation, and Cole was there with his long-coupled, limber-legged, swaggering-gaited horse. Out of derision, several sports bantered Cole for a race, to which he readily consented, amid the hoots of the crowd. A long-haired, wealthy planter, with a clean cut and noted racer of the neighborhood, was Cole's antagonist. The amount of the stakes was $1,000 which was deposited with a man on the ground, an entire stranger to Cole, but he never anticipated any unfairness.

Everything being in readiness, the horses were brought up to the starting point. Cole riding his own horse, and they were sent off fairly together. It was a half-mile stretch over an excellent track and for the first quarter the animals kept neck and neck, but on the last quarter Cole's horse gathered up his coupling, straightened himself, and was throwing dust in the eyes of his antagonist, winning in fine style, when a fellow jumped out in front of Cole's horse and threw a red blanket across the track. The result was, what the fellow anticipated. Cole's horse broke the track and cut across the open field, thereby losing the race.

Cole did not say a word to the jockey, but, reining up his horse, he rode back to the starting point and claimed a foul. The crowd made sport of his claim, derided his horse and flung epithets at him. Seeing that it was the intention of the racers to defraud him. Cole first appealed vainly to the judges and then to the stake-holder; the latter party laughed in his face and then delivered the stakes to the Southerner, whose horse had won by such outrageous trickery. Cole's face grew paler than usual, his brow lowered and his lips became nervous; it was evident there was a struggle within him and that there was just a moment of irresolution. He remained perfectly still on his horse for nearly a minute, receiving the derisive banters of the crowd, and then he turned partly in the saddle, drew two navy revolvers and opened fire; the first shot killed the stake-holder, and the two judges fell next under his steady aim, while in quick succession, five others received terrible wounds, from which three of them never recovered.

The laugh quickly faded from the lips of those who thought they were plucking a harmless and ignorant Missourian, and in the place of funds for a rollicking spree, there were dead men awaiting burial, and others ready for, the surgeon's care.

After the slaughter Cole rode swiftly away, with none to pursue him, and made direct for Missouri, which he reached in the latter part of June, and directly thereafter went to California in company with Frank James.

# ROBBING THE GALLATIN, MISSOURI, BANK.

More than eighteen months elapsed after the Russellville robbery before the desperate bandits were again heard of by the public. Cole Younger and Frank James spent more than one year of this time in California with their relatives. Their deeds were so far forgotten as to be remembered only in the traditions of what were called "stirring times." The country banks had relaxed their vigilance, and detectives, anxious to pluck honors by bringing noted criminals to justice, looked no longer toward the border bandits. Suddenly, and with a surprise which shook society like a social earthquake, the outlaws returned to their old haunts in Missouri, and descended like some terrible avalanche upon the Daviess County Savings Bank at Gallatin. It was but a fragment of the old crowd, however, Cole Younger and the James Boys, the most desperate trio that guerrilla warfare ever gave birth to.

It was on the 7th of December, 1869, when the three rode leisurely into Gallatin and stopped in front of the bank. Cole and Jesse dismounted, leaving Frank with the horses and to keep the outside clear of interference. In the bank, at the time, was a young man named McDowell making a deposit, and Capt. John W. Sheets, the cashier. Jesse James threw a one hundred dollar bill on the counter and asked the cashier to give him small change in return. Capt. Sheets took the bill, walked back to the safe, took out a handful of money, and, returning to the counter, was in the act of counting out the change, when Cole Younger suddenly thrust a navy revolver forward and commanded the cashier to surrender to them the keys of the inner doors of the safe, the outer ones being open. Before the startled McDowell could recover from his astonishment, he found the deadly revolver of Jesse James covering his person, and was forced to consider himself a prisoner. Cole Younger went behind the counter, plundered the safe and till, and secured in all about seven hundred dollars in currency. After rifling the safe, there was a whispered consultation, and the next moment Jesse James turned and deliberately shot Capt. Sheets dead. Meantime one or two persons who had come to the bank on business had been driven away by the confederate outside, and this, together with the sound of the pistol shots, had caused an alarm to be given. The whole transaction occupied but a few minutes, but by the time the robbers emerged from the bank, a dozen citizens had snatched up various weapons and were moving up the street toward the bank. Frank James called out to his comrades, his cry being answered by the immediate appearance of Jesse and Cole, who rushed out of the bank. The horses, spirited animals, were headed for flight, and affrighted by the shouts of the advancing crowd, Jesse's horse gave a plunge just as he, with one foot in the stirrup, had made an effort to mount. The suddenness of the horse's movement completely discomfited the robber, who fell to the ground and was dragged about thirty feet head downwards with one heel fast in the stirrup. By that time, however, he succeeded in disengaging himself. For a second he lay prone on the ground, while the fractious steed went careering away in the distance. The crowd of citizens began to open a lively fusillade, but Frank James instantly wheeled and rode back to his dismounted brother, who leaped up behind him, and away they went together. Less than ten minutes had elapsed when the citizens were mounted in pursuit, and they must soon have overtaken the overloaded horse that was carrying double. It so happened, however, that about a mile southwest of town the fugitives met Mr. Dan Smoot riding an excellent saddle-horse. Without a moment's hesitation they rode up to him, and with the muzzle of a revolver an inch from his nose, requested him to dismount. Of course he took to the bush with great alacrity, and the three bandits were once more thoroughly equipped. They appeared to have had little fear for the result after this. Between Gallatin and Kidder they talked with several persons, boasting of what they had done. On nearing Kidder they met Rev. Mr. Helm, a Methodist minister. They pressed him into service by the use of the usual persuasion, the revolver, and made him guide them around so that they could avoid the town. On leaving him one of them told Mr. Helm that he was Bill Anderson's brother, and that he killed S. P. Cox, if he hadn't made a mistake in the man. He claimed that this was an act of vengeance for the death of his brother Bill.

The pursuing posse followed hot upon the heels of the fugitives, who were once or twice almost in sight. About six miles south of Kidder they took to the woods, going toward the Missouri river, and there their woodcraft and the approach of night enabled them to escape. The horse which had escaped and so nearly killed Jesse in front of the bank, was held by the sheriff of Daviess county. The escaping robbers were traced across into Clay county, and the abandoned horse, according to an account in the

Kansas City Times, of December 16, 1869, was fully identified as the property of "a young man named James, whose mother and step-father live about four miles from Centreville, Clay county, near the Cameron branch of the Hannibal and St. Joe Railroad." The account adds that "both he and his brother are desperate men, having had much experience in horse and revolver work." The most careful inquiry was made in order to leave no question as to the identity of the robbers, and it is still held that there was no doubt about Frank and Jesse James and Cole Younger being the trio.

As soon as it was definitely ascertained who the men were and where they lived, two of the citizens of Gallatin, thoroughly armed and mounted, rode away to Liberty, Clay county, where they called on Mr. Tomlinson, the deputy sheriff, and stated what they knew about the three outlaws, and what they had done in Gallatin. Tomlinson, accompanied by his son and the two pursuers from Gallatin, started at once for Dr. Samuels' house, the step-father of the brothers James. This house is some 20 miles from Liberty. Approaching it, some strategy was displayed. The Gallatin detachment watching it from the side next the woods, the Liberty detachment — father and son — dismounted at the gate in front of the house and walked very deliberately up to the door. Before reaching it, however, a little negro boy ran past them and on to the stable, and just as he got there, the door opened suddenly, and out dashed the two brothers on splendid horses, with pistols drawn, and took the lot fence at a swinging gallop. The Gallatin party, from the fence above, opened fire on sight; the sheriff and his son followed suit; the brothers joined in at intervals, and then the chase began. To mount and away in pursuit was with Tomlinson but the work of a few seconds, and he dashed on after the robbers. His horse alone of all the horses ridden in pursuit would take the fence, and so while the rest of the party were dismounting and pulling off top rails, Mr. Tomlinson was riding like the wind after the two brothers. He gained upon them, well mounted as they were. He fired several times at them and they at him, but the rate of speed was too great for accuracy. Carried on by the ardor of the chase, Mr. Tomlinson soon found himself far in advance of the supporting column and, in fact, hotly pursuing two desperadoes with no weapon to rely upon except an empty revolver. Just what happened will probably never be known, as there were no witnesses except the principals. A short time afterward, however, Mr. T. came back to Dr. Samuels' house on foot, having evidently made a forced march through the brush. Reborrowed a horse and started for Centreville. He had hardly been gone ten minutes, when the two James boys returned to the house, and on learning that he had had the cheek to come back there, they went after him, swearing they would kill him. They missed him, however. The horse he had first ridden was afterward found shot dead. Tomlinson reached Liberty about ten o'clock that night, and found the town in considerable excitement over the report that he had been killed. His posse having lost track of him, had returned to Liberty and circulated the report.

Tomlinson's story about the affair was that he found he could not hit the boys from a running horse, and so he dismounted to get one deliberate shot. The outlaws subsequently told some of their friends that when they found only one man close to them they turned on him and killed his horse, whereupon he plunged into a thicket, and they were willing enough to let him get away, but they had no idea he would go to their home for a fresh horse. Of course the whole country turned out after this, to catch the Jameses, but they were not caught. The robbery was, perhaps, the most remarkable of all that have been done by the Missouri bandits, partly because only three men were engaged in it, and partly, because of the utter wantonness of the murder committed.

In justice to Cole Younger, let it be said, that he not only denied any participation in this outrage, but there are hundreds of persons who have announced their readiness to make oath that Cole was not in Missouri at the time of the robbery. Both the James boys also offered to prove alibis, but it is almost certain they were the perpetrators of the pillage and murder. The proof is much less convincing respecting Cole's participation. The account of the robbery as here given, is in conformity with the generally accepted belief of the people in and about Gallatin.

# THE HANGING OF JOHN YOUNGER.

After the first charges of robbery were preferred against Cole and James Younger, there was no time in which they could neglect a vigilant watch, for detectives were in constant pursuit, and armed bands of vindictive border residents were almost constantly prowling about the Younger residence, with the hope of catching Cole, especially. In the early part of 1870, only a few months before the death of Mrs. Younger, a squad of twelve men, supposed to be Kansas vigilants, stole upon the Younger residence during the night, in pursuance of information received that Cole and Jim were at home. Upon forcibly entering the house, they found only John Younger and his sisters ministering to the needs of their dying mother. The scene was one of extraordinary sadness and would have caused, it would seem, the most callous heart to bleed with sympathy. Mrs. Younger had suffered so much by the havoc of war and the passions of infamous men, that her health gave way and she fell a victim to that slow, but certain destroyer, consumption. When the squad entered the house with rattling spurs and aspects fiercer than the arms they bore, the wretched mother lay like one in the grasp of death; the sunken eyes, hectic cheeks and emaciated form, around which gathered those who realized how soon they would be motherless, was that "touch of nature which makes the whole world kin."

Singular as it appears, the armed posse took no heed of the tread of death which might have been heard in the room; their aspects were not softened by sympathy, and their purpose was inflexible; they meant to kill. The house was examined but no traces of Cole or Jim Younger were discovered; demands made upon John and his sisters respecting the whereabouts of their outlaw brothers, were, of course, treated with ignorance. But the squad, determined not to be deceived, forcibly took John away from the bedside of his mother and carried him to the barn; here they attempted to extort from him the information they sought, first by threats, and failing in this they resorted to torture. A noose was thrown around the unfortunate boy's neck and run over a rafter; he was then drawn up and left suspended until his face grew black. The poor fellow was then let down and again asked to reveal the hiding place of his brothers. Still declaring that he did not know, the squad again suspended him as before; three times this cruel treatment was repeated; the last time he was allowed to hang so long that the rope lacerated his neck, and when they let him down he was unconscious. After recovering somewhat, the now infuriated mob had recourse to their knives; with these they cut and slashed the boy, finally leaving him apparently dead. For several hours he lay unconscious and bleeding in the barn before his sisters discovered him, they being compelled to remain in the house when their brother was carried away.

It was several weeks before John recovered from the wounds he had received, and during his convalescence Mrs. Younger died, and then the family was indeed wrecked. To escape further persecution, John Younger went to Texas where his other brothers had preceded him some time before, and for a short time he clerked in a grocery store in Dallas.

# THE MURDER OF SHERIFF NICHOLS.

During his residence in Texas, John Younger formed the acquaintance of a large number of questionable characters, and under their influence he was led into the commission of a crime which he has bitterly repented of a thousand times. The particulars concerning the murder of the sheriff of Dallas county, by John Younger, have been given so many times and with such variance that it is impossible now to relate the circumstances without incorporating some misstatements. John Younger's story makes the deed one of justifiable homicide, while others declare it to have been a cold-blooded murder. In the absence of a reasonable motive, it is impossible for the writer to believe that the murder was committed without cause. Following is believed to be the most reliable version:

On the night of January 15, 1871, John Younger, in company with several associates, was in a saloon in Dallas kept by Joe Krueger; the crowd had been drinking rather freely, and their conversation finally turned on who was the best pistol shot in the party. In the saloon at the time was an old besotted wretch who went by the euphonious title of "Old Blue;" whiskey had destroyed his manhood and produced a physical wreck. His only desire was for whiskey, and to obtain this he would hesitate at nothing.

John Younger professed to be a crack shot with a pistol, and at length bet the crowd a treat that he could shoot a pipe out of "Old Blue's" mouth at the space of ten steps. The old fellow was sitting in a chair half drunk when the proposition was made, and shook his head in doubt but, said nothing. One of the men accepted the bet, and to get "Old Blue" to stand the fire, he was given two glasses full of whiskey. The space was measured off in the saloon, and the old sot was propped up in the corner with a pipe in his mouth, his head had been steadied by lying back between two beer kegs. John Younger then took position and, aiming as deliberately as his condition would allow, fired. "Old Blue" gave a snort as the bullet cut off the end of his nose and the blood streamed from the wound in great profusion. He yelled murder, and nothing would pacify him, not even the offer of a barrel of whiskey. The crowd soon after broke up and went home, leaving the old man to take care of himself.

On the following day, at the suggestion of some official persons, "Old Blue" swore out a warrant against John Younger, charging him with attempt to commit murder. The sheriff of the county, Capt. S. W. Nichols, who was a former resident of Missouri and an officer in the Confederate service, took the warrant himself and served it on Younger. John received the sheriff very affably, but when the warrant for arrest was read, he began to reflect seriously about submitting. The reputation of the Younger Boys was well known in Texas, and John concluded at once that if he became a prisoner that other charges would be preferred against him by his enemies.

Contemplating his position for a moment, John Younger made answer: "All right, Captain, just as quick as I get my breakfast I'll come over to your office."

This reply did not exactly satisfy the sheriff, though he said nothing, concluding to remain and watch the house until Younger came out, at the same time entertaining fears that some trouble was imminent. Back of the place where John was boarding, there was a livery stable, and after eating his breakfast, he passed out at the back way and had reached the stable, where he inquired for a horse, when the sheriff espied him. As he ran, Nichols drew his pistol and commanded John to halt, but, instead of obeying, Younger ran through the stable and was passing out at the rear door, when the sheriff fired at him. Finding himself headed off by a blind alley, John turned and, drawing his pistol, forbid the further approach of the sheriff. By this time considerable excitement had been created and a merchant of the place seized a loaded shot-gun and joined in the pursuit. Finding escape impossible, while the sheriff was shooting at him from time to time. Younger at length put out his pistol and shot Nichols through the heart, killing him instantly; the merchant, whose name cannot now be recalled, then discharged his gun at John, sending a load of fine shot into his shoulder. The next moment the merchant lay writhing with a pistol ball in his breast, while John ran back through a small crowd and, taking a horse that was standing hitched to a fence, he mounted and rode off. Some hours afterward a posse of citizens went in search of the fugitive and followed him for more than one hundred miles, but he escaped and came north to St. Clair county. Mo., where, after obtaining some money, he went to California. He remained in Los Angeles for several months, unable to find any profitable employment, and receiving a request from his brother Cole to return, he started back by rail. On the route home, a detective sought to accomplish his arrest and there was an exchange of shots in the car when the train was twelve miles west of Laramie. The detective was shot through the arm, while John, being unhurt, leaped from the running train, seriously spraining his right ankle in the fall. He made his way on foot for several miles and finally fell in with a wagon train for Denver. From that city he reached home after a journey replete with misfortunes, for, having no money, he was repeatedly put off the train and more than one-third the distance he was compelled to walk in shoes so badly worn that they could scarcely be kept on his feet.

After reaching home, John joined his two brothers. Cole and Jim, and afterward was with them in their raids until his death in 1874.

# THE CORYDON, IOWA, BANK ROBBERY.

The bank-raiding outlaws went into seclusion after the Gallatin robbery, spending another eighteen months in Texas and their impregnable cave in Jackson county, Missouri. They had a well-defined policy of action by which they were guided in their social intercourse as well as in their dangerous adventures. Secret communication was kept up when the band was divided, and each one was always on the alert for special opportunities in the practice of their peculiar profession.

After a long period of idleness and plotting, the reorganized band, consisting of the two James boys, Cole and Jim Younger, Clell Miller, Jim White and one other, whose identity has never been conclusively established, seven in all, decided to visit Iowa and plunder the bank of Obocock Bros, in Corydon. On the 3rd of June, 1871, the seven outlaws, well mounted and armed, came trooping into the town, like so many countrymen hastening to the political meeting then in progress in the public square. They halted before the bank and three of the party dismounted, while the remaining four stood guard on the outside. The dismounted trio entered the bank, very quietly, and, finding no one inside but the cashier, it being high noon, he was confronted by three heavy revolvers and then bound hand and foot. This was a singular act which the bandits never before or since attempted, and their purpose is not yet apparent, for they obtained the keys of the safe without trouble, and plundered it of nearly $40,000, one of the largest hauls, if not the largest, they had ever made up to that time.

After completing the robbery and placing their treasure in a sack, the three emerged from the bank and, mounting their horses, the entire party masked themselves with handkerchiefs and rode over to the political meeting, which was being addressed by Henry Clay Dean, where Jesse James asked pardon of the speaker for interrupting him a few moments. Mr. Dean graciously gave way when Jesse, still sitting astride his horse With the other bandits by his side, spoke as follows: "Well, you've been having your fun and we've been having ours. You needn't go into hysterics when I tell you that we've just been down to the bank and robbed it of every dollar in the till. If you'll go down there now you'll find the cashier tied and then if you want any of us, why, just come down and take us. Thank you for your attention." At the conclusion of this strange speech the seven dare-devils set up a wild yell, lifted their hats and sped away southward. The crowd thought the confession was only a plan to break up the meeting, but a few minutes served to prove the truth of Jesse's words.

After discovering the robbery there were hasty preparations for pursuit, and a posse of a dozen men, headed by the sheriff, dashed off in reckless haste to capture the bandits. On the second day the outlaws were overtaken in Daviess county, Mo., and a fight ensued, but the citizens were forced to give way without inflicting any damage on the bold marauders. Others joined in the chase, however, and the trail was followed into Clay county and then into Jackson, where the track faded out suddenly.

The Kansas City detectives continued to search for the perpetrators of the robbery and two months afterward they arrested Clell Miller in Clay county and took him back to Iowa on a requisition. He was tried at Corydon in November, 1872, the court proceedings lasting from Monday, November 10th until the Friday following, when, owing to the insufficiency of the identification evidence, he was discharged; the mask he wore had saved him.

The Younger and James Boys stoutly protested their innocence and referred to scores of parties in the counties of Clay and Jackson to prove their presence in certain places, at the date of the robbery. The accepted belief, however, is that the outrage was perpetrated by the individuals named in this account; the alibi had become a subterfuge altogether too flimsy.

# THE COLUMBIA, KENTUCKY, BANK ROBBERY.

The outlaws spent several months in their well-furnished cave in Jackson county, living a life of elegant ease, enjoying all the comforts liberal wealth could purchase. Tired, at last, of hilarious idleness, the James and Younger Boys concluded to pay another visit to their friends and relatives in Kentucky. Having plenty of money they divided with their poorer kinship in Nelson county, and sporting until their natures grew restless for new adventures, they planned the pillage of the Deposit Bank at Columbia. First providing themselves with the purest blooded horses they could purchase, and completing every detail for a profitable ride, the three Younger brothers and the James Boys set out for Columbia.

On the 29th of April, 1872, the five daring outlaws rode into Columbia by different roads, coming together in the public square at 2:30 o'clock in the afternoon. Scarcely had they met when John and Jim Younger dashed down the street yelling and firing their pistols at every person seen abroad, while Cole and the two James Boys rode directly to the bank and entered with drawn pistols. In the bank at the time was the cashier, Hon. R. A. C. Martin, James Garnett and Mr. Dalrymple. A demand was made on the cashier for the safe keys, which being refused, one of the outlaws shot him dead. The other gentlemen in the bank made a hasty exit, leaving the bandits in undisturbed possession. Being unable to effect an entrance into the safe, the robbers were compelled to content themselves with the currency they found in the drawers, amounting to about two hundred dollars; they then remounted their horses and the gang galloped away southward. On the same afternoon of the robbery, fifteen men, with such horses and arms as they could hastily secure, started out after the bandits, while telegrams were sent in every direction with the hope of heading them off. Others joined in the chase, and the trail was followed pertinaciously through Kentucky and several hundred miles in Tennessee, but the outlaws gained the dense coverts and recesses of the Cumberland Mountains where pursuit ended. The shooting of the cashier has been charged to Frank James, but this is merely supposition. It is almost certain that Cole Younger did not commit the murder, because of his well known aversion to the adoption of such expedients to effect a robbery; Cole would try intimidation, but his nature revolted at murder except where the conditions were equally divided, and it was life staked against life.

# A DARING RAID AT THE KANSAS CITY FAIR.

The outlaws returned to Missouri after their last raid in Kentucky, and spent several months in their comfortably fitted up cave in Jackson county. Jesse and Frank James were frequent visitors at their mother's house, and Cole and John Younger were not infrequent guests at the same residence. All the Younger brothers were seen together when they attended the Sny Bar church on the second Sunday in August, and they took no means to hide their identity. In the September following, 1872, the Kansas City Fair was held, beginning on the 23d; the attendance was very large, one of the special attractions being the renowned horse Ethan Allen, which was advertised to trot against a running mate on Thursday, the 26th. At this time the writer was a reporter on the Kansas City Journal, and was performing special duties at the fair, occupying a position which afforded every facility for learning full particulars of the incident about to be related.

When Thursday, which is always the "big day" of the Exposition, arrived, every incoming train poured hundreds of new arrivals into the city. The streets were literally jammed during the early morning hours, and by nine o'clock the stream of humanity began to flow toward the fair grounds. It was, indeed, a big day for both the city and the fair association. By one o'clock in the afternoon there was scarcely standing-room about the race course or the buildings containing exhibition articles. Ethan Allen was brought out and shown to the thousands occupying the amphitheatre, and then the pool selling began on the other races to take place after the noted horse had exhibited his speed. I can never forget the excitement manifested by the crowd; not that there we're any rows or disturbances, but the gathering was so great, and there was such an unusual disposition to bet, both on Ethan Allen's time, and the combinations in the pool, that the noise was like Pandemonium on election day.

At three o'clock the great horse appeared in harness in the ring, and when he was sent off the most deafening cries arose from the crowd and continued until the mile was finished, in 2:18, I believe. After this there was a gradual dispersion of the vast assemblage, numbering more than thirty thousand persons, and the streets leading to the city were filled with returning people.

At four o'clock in the afternoon, Mr. Hall, the secretary and treasurer of the Fair Association, completed counting the receipts of the day and, in response to a question from the writer, he stated that the day's revenue was only a fraction less than $10,000. This money he placed in a large tin box, which he instructed his assistant to carry to the First National Bank for deposit. The young man left the secretary's headquarters about ten minutes after four o'clock, and in fifteen minutes afterward a big rush toward the gates indicated that some unusual incident had occurred. The writer ran rapidly in the direction taken by the crowd, and at the entrance gates, which are more than a quarter of a mile from the main buildings, he soon learned the cause of so much excitement. As the young man with the treasure box was passing through the gate, three horsemen rode swiftly up to him, and one of them leaping to the ground, snatched the box and handed it to his mounted companion. The young man shouted lustily for help, and though he was surrounded by dozens of men leaving the grounds, no one seemed to think of attempting to arrest the robbers. The three mounted outlaws rode through the crowd with such recklessness, that a little girl, about ten years of age, was badly trampled, but not fatally injured, her left hip being lacerated severely. As the bandits repeatedly fired their pistols, for a time it was thought the little girl was struck by a bullet, but this accident was the only casualty. Before the hundreds of surprised witnesses of the struggle could recover from their fright, the three daring highwaymen sped away like the wind, carrying the $10,000 with them.

The excitement following the robbery was intense, and every one seemed to have distinct suspicions as to who the bandits were. The police, detectives, and the sheriff with several deputized citizens, went in pursuit of the robbers before night approached, and they had no difficulty in following the trail for a distance of ten miles, when the tracks faded like fog lifted by a heavy wind; the outlaws had entered their mysterious cave and, while counting their sudden gain, laughed at the foiled pursuers.

From confessions since made by members of the gang, it has been definitely ascertained that the three desperate outlaws were Jesse and Frank James and Bob Younger, and that the party who dismounted and grabbed the cash box, was Jesse James.

Some time after the robbery, the latter wrote a card, which was published in the Kansas City Times, denying his connection with the robbery, and accused Cole Younger of acting the principal part in the daring outrage, but regardless of his proffered proof of an alibi, the perpetrators were certainly the three named; at least the most satisfactory evidence obtainable so indicates.

# THE STE. GENEVIEVE, MO., BANK ROBBERY.

Every robbery thus far had been consummated with such signal success, that the outlaws could not long remain idle, for the love of money increased with its accumulation, just as the love of adventure grew greater with successful accomplishment. Before the winter ended, Jim Younger and Frank James left their hiding place in Jackson county and made a trip through the northwest, going through Omaha and as far west as Cheyenne, where they remained for a considerable time prospecting for opportunities. They both had relatives in California, and as shipments of gold over the Union Pacific Railroad from San Francisco were frequent, the purpose of the two bandits was, doubtless, to ascertain the date of contemplated express shipments of treasure. During their stay in Cheyenne, Cole and Bob Younger, Jesse James, Bill Chadwell, alias Styles, and Clell Miller, conceived and definitely arranged a plan to rob the Savings Association at Ste. Genevieve, Missouri. In pursuance of their arrangements, the five bandits left Jackson county about the 1st of May, 1873, and stopped a short time at a country place a few miles south of Springfield. From here they went to Bismarck, on the Iron Mountain Railroad, but remained there only one day. From this latter point they rode through Ste. Genevieve county and on the morning of May twenty-seventh, the five outlaws appeared in the old Catholic town, three entering from the south and two from the north.

It was shortly after nine o'clock when the bandits made their appearance, and as three of them entered the bank they found no one inside except the cashier, O. D. Harris, Esq., and a son of Hon. Firman A. Rozier, the president. No time was given for parley; the robbers presented their pistols at the cashier and commanded him to open the safe. Young Rozier comprehended the situation at once, and as none of the pistols were covering him, he ran down the steps and through the street rapidly, calling for help. The two bandits who stood guard outside fired three times at the fleeing boy, one bullet passing through his coat, but doing no bodily injury. Mr. Harris appreciating the critical position he occupied, accepted the more sensible alternative and opened the safe door, permitting the outlaws to secure all the funds then in the bank, amounting to four thousand one hundred dollars. This money, much of which was silver, they threw into a sack, and mounting their horses decamped. Before getting out of town the bandit who carried the sack, by some means, let his treasure fall to the ground, which necessitated his return for it. All the five robbers came together here, and four of them halted in the road while the fifth one dismounted for the treasure sack; in the attempt to remount, his horse became frightened and broke away, running some distance north. At this juncture a German came riding into town, and the mounted bandits by direful threats compelled him to ride after and secure the fugitive horse, which he accomplished after considerable delay. In the meantime a posse of citizens gathered, and obtaining horses quickly, they went in pursuit of the robbers, whom they came up with within a mile of the town. There was an exchange of shots which halted the citizens, and after this the outlaws were not again approached.

The bold desperadoes, in order to exasperate the authorities, it would appear, marked their trail by leaving sign boards in their wake on which they would inscribe the day and hour they were at the spot indicated by the board. On the 30th of May the robbers rode into Hermann, Missouri, and stopped for dinner, telling the people of the place who they were, and performing other dare-devil acts which set the authorities after them in a state of fury. The chase continued for weeks, it being joined in by several detectives from Chicago and St. Louis, who arrested dozens of "suspicious characters" only to find they had the wrong men. It was thus the chase ended, as all the other attempts to arrest the bandits had terminated.

The Savings Association at Ste. Genevieve was one of the strongest banks in the State, carrying a deposit of over one hundred thousand dollars continually during the period of its active existence. At the time of the raid the bank was winding up its business, and to facilitate this, the capital and funds were deposited with the Merchants' Bank of St. Louis, and all the deposits had been drawn out. But for this fact the robbery would have resulted, as the bandits, no doubt, anticipated, in a magnificent appropriation.

# ROBBING A TRAIN IN IOWA.

When the five outlaws reached Jackson county from Ste. Genevieve, they found Frank James and Jim Younger in waiting with a plan perfected for collecting treasure which they had learned would be shipped over the Union Pacific Railroad, reaching Omaha on the morning of July 21st. How they obtained this information can only be conjectured from facts already given. Their trip to Cheyenne, therefore, had resulted very satisfactorily, and the band made immediate preparations to profit by the news. Accordingly, on the 12th of July, the party of seven left their secret haunts and mounted on excellent horses, they set out for the neighborhood of Council Bluffs, reaching their destination about the 18th. Frank James and Cole Younger visited Omaha to learn what they could respecting the treasure which was expected, and by what road it would be sent east from Council Bluffs. They returned to their waiting comrades on the 21st, and in the afternoon arrangements were made for wrecking the evening passenger train on the Chicago, Rock Island & Pacific Railroad. The spot selected for this purpose was about five miles west of Adair, a small town in Adair county, where there is a sharp curve in the road which obscures the rails sixty yards in advance of the engine. The outlaws hitched their horses some distance from the track out of sight from the train, and procuring a spike-bar loosened one of the rails. To this loose rail they tied a rope leading several yards out into the grass, where they concealed themselves. The passenger train consisted of seven coaches, including the two sleepers, and was due at the point of ambush at 8:30 p. m. John Rafferty was in charge of the engine and was looking sharply along the curve when he saw the rail move out of place. He instantly reversed the lever, but the distance was so short, while the momentum of the train was so great, that the engine plunged through the break and turned over, while the coaches piled on top of one another in direful confusion. The engineer was instantly killed and a dozen passengers seriously injured. Notwithstanding this result, the robbers quickly boarded the wreck, two of them entering the express car, while the others forced the excited and demoralized passengers to deliver up all their money and valuables. The express messenger was made to open the safe and give the bandits what money he had in charge, but the amount was small, consisting of about three thousand dollars. From the passengers nearly as much more was obtained. This was a bitter disappointment to the outlaws, for they confidently expected to find not less than fifty thousand dollars in gold, as reported. Fortunately the bandits were twelve hours too soon, as on the following day the express carried over the same road seventy-five thousand dollars in gold.

After securing all the booty possible, the seven daring wreckers waved their hats and shouted farewell to their victims, and gaining their horses, they rode away to the south.

The excitement created over this dreadful outrage was very great and hundreds volunteered to assist in apprehending the desperadoes. The trail led straight through Missouri and to the Missouri river, where there was unmistakable evidence that the outlaws swam the stream with their horses. Following the track on the other side, the band was followed into Jackson county, where, as usual, every trace disappeared. A party of detectives went down to Monegaw springs in search of the outlaws and found Jesse James and two of the Younger Boys, but they made no effort to bring them away and were glad to escape themselves alive.

Cole Younger has always strenuously denied any participation in the wrecking of the train, and the writer confesses to a reluctance in believing he was present. The facts, as gathered from available sources, sometimes doubtful, are given here without any pretention to positiveness. The narrative is in accordance with the generally accepted belief.

On the day after the robbery five of the bandits, or, at least, believed to be them, took dinner at the house of a farmer named Stuckeye, in Ringgold county. He described these men as follows:

No. 1. Seemed to be a kind of leader; five feet seven or eight inches tall, light hair, blue eyes, heavy sandy whiskers, broad shoulders, short nose, a little turned up; high, broad forehead; looked to be a well-educated man not used to work; age, thirty-six to forty.

No. 2. Tall and lithe, with light complexion, high forehead, light brown hair, long, light whiskers, almost sandy, long, slender hands that certainly had not done much hard work, nose a prominent Roman. He was very polite and talked but little. Looked thirty-six years old.

No. 3. Slender, five feet nine or ten inches tall, hair cut short and of a light brown color, straight nose, uncouth and sarcastic in speech, brown eyes, and wearing a hard, dissipated countenance. Middle-aged, and wore dark clothes.

No. 4. Dark complexion, dark hair, clean shaved, five feet eight inches tall, heavy set, straight, black eyes, straight nose, good looking, but appeared dissipated. Middle-aged, and wore light pants, hat and vest and dark coat.

No. 5. Five feet ten inches tall, large, broad shoulders, straight, blue eyes, reddish whiskers. Roman nose. Middle-aged, and very pleasant in appearance.

These descriptions answer for Frank and Jesse James, Clell Miller and Jim and Bob Younger; where the other two bandits were at this time, it is difficult to surmise, especially since it is positively known that the seven were together when they rode through Missouri.

Jack Bishop, in a card in the Kansas City Times, accused Ike Flannery of being one of the band, but this accusation might have readily proceeded from some prejudice or other motive. The public will, perhaps, never learn positively each member of the band that wrecked the passenger train, for the act was so disgraceful and monstrous, displaying neither bravery nor cunning, that circumstances can hardly induce any of the party to make a confession of the crime and name his accomplices.

# THE HOT SPRINGS STAGE ROBBERY.

After the train wrecking in Iowa there was another long period of inactivity among the bandits. The James and Younger Boys were frequently seen by intimate acquaintances in Jackson and Clay counties; they also spent a considerable time in Texas, but committed no new depredations until the beginning of 1874. By this time their money was probably well nigh exhausted, as all the band were known to be high livers during their periods of plenty. During the holidays of 1873, the outlaws proposed other schemes for plunder, and by New Year's day of 1874, they had perfected their plans for three robberies, which were accomplished according to programme. When they left their haunts. Bob Younger and Jesse James went to Louisiana, while Frank James, Cole and Jim Younger, Arthur McCoy and Clell Miller remained together to carry out their designs for robbing the stage running between Malvern and Hot Springs, Arkansas. On the 15th of January, the five bandits left Hot Springs, where they had remained the previous night, and secreted themselves near the stage roadside, five miles east of the town. At eleven o'clock in the forenoon, the heavy Concord stage with two ambulances and fourteen passengers, came lumbering over the rough road enroute for the Springs. When the stage came nearly abreast of the robbers, they suddenly rose out of their hiding-place and, presenting their pistols, sternly commanded the driver to halt. Frank James acted as leader and was the one who gave the order. The driver, thoroughly frightened by the appearance of the bandits, drew rein quickly and became a quiet spectator of the proceedings that followed.

The outlaws soon informed the astonished passengers the occasion for such authoritative actions on their part, by ordering the immediate vacating of the vehicles. Obedience became a stern necessity under the pressure of so many deadly appearing weapons, and when the passengers stepped out, they were ordered to form a line along the road, then the most interesting part of the programme began to take place.

Jim Younger and Clell Miller acted as examining experts, while the other outlaws maintained guard. To more thoroughly intimidate the already almost insensible travelers, a conversation was carried on between the bandits, well calculated to freeze the slow-flowing blood of their victims. Each individual was robbed of every cent that could be found and their watches, were also appropriated. A Mr. Taylor, of Boston, who had the unmistakable appearance of a "down caster," was persecuted by the threats made against his life, and ex-Governor Burbank, of Dakotah, was about to be executed on the suspicion that he was a detective, but bloodshed was averted; it may never have been contemplated, and the threats were probably intended only to frighten.

One of the passengers betrayed a Southern nativity by his speech, and one of the bandits asked him if he had been in the Southern army; receiving an affirmative reply, together with satisfying information concerning his regiment and company, the outlaws returned the money and valuables taken from him. After completing the robbery and securing about $4,000, Cole Younger made a brief explanation of the causes which led the band to the commission of such iniquities. He referred to the remorseless manner in which he and his parents had been harassed and despoiled by jayhawkers, and how he had been pursued after the war until forced to become an outlaw. The entire band spoke very vindictively about Pinkerton's detectives and made many threats of vengeance. They then very courteously bade their victims an adieu, mounted their horses and soon disappeared over the hills.

When the stage reached Hot Springs, a full report of the robbery was made, but owing to the almost inaccessible condition of the surrounding country, little or no effort was made to capture the highwaymen.

# ROBBING A TRAIN AT GAD'S HILL.

Finding that the stage robbery had created little excitement, the band did not delay long in accomplishing the second plan they had arranged one month before in Jackson county. After taking a northwest direction and going into a familiar settlement in southern Missouri near the Arkansas line, they took a resting spell of nearly two weeks, and then rode to Gad's Hill, a small station on the Iron Mountain Railroad in Wayne county, Missouri. They made hasty preparations to rob the Little Rock express train, which was due at Gad's Hill shortly before six o'clock p. m. The station contained a population of not more than a dozen persons, and the country about was very sparsely settled, so that no danger of interference was anticipated from the neighborhood. Their first precaution was to make a prisoner of the station agent and the five other men found about the station. The switch was then turned so as to force a stoppage of the train should it attempt to pass by. Clell Miller then secured the signal flag and planted it in the center of the tracks after which the bandits awaited the coming of their victims. Promptly on time the train rattled along the track, and the engineer seeing the flag closed the throttle valve and brought the heavy passenger coaches to a standstill alongside the little platform. The conductor, Mr. Alvord, stepped off one of the cars to ascertain the cause of the signal, but at the same moment he was confronted by a revolver in the hands of Frank James and made to surrender. The outlaws were then posted, one on each side of the train, another covering the engineer and prisoners, while the other two went through the coaches, and by fierce threats and more dangerous revolvers compelled all the passengers in the first-class car and the sleepers to disgorge their money and valuables. After completing the robbery of the passengers, the express car was next raided, obtaining from the safe one thousand and eighty dollars, and then the mail bags were cut open and rifled, one registered letter being secured which contained two thousand dollars in currency. The money and valuables obtained aggregated nearly twelve thousand dollars. None of the bandits entered the second-class cars, saying they were only after the "plug hat" crowd. Southern men, they also passed over, when convinced of the fact. During the robbery the band talked constantly, but were always vigilant.

All of them wore masks made of calico with holes cut for the eyes. Only one of them had an overcoat, and it was this one who attended to the switch and guarded the prisoners. When he fixed the forward switch he had thrown his overcoat down on the track. After the robbery was over they brought the train men out, put them on the train and told them to pull out. After the train started, one of them happened to discover that the overcoat was still lying on the track, when he instantly made the engineer stop until the fellow could go and get it. The amount obtained from the passengers was nearly two thousand dollars. As usual, there was a great deal of guessing as to who the robbers were. Entirely reliable parties who had known all the men named, declared positively that two of the Youngers, that is. Cole and Bob, or Cole and Jim, were with Arthur McCoy and Bill Greenwood and another man in the vicinity for a day or two before the robbery. That they were the same party who had been chased up from Hot Springs, and that an hour before they went to the station they all had blue overcoats on. Other circumstances strengthened the belief that these were the men, and of course, one of the James Boys was put in for the fifth man.

Before leaving, the robbers left the following flash account of the affair with one of the train men:

"The most daring on record — the southbound train on the Iron Mountain Railroad was robbed here this evening by five heavily armed men, and robbed of — dollars. The robbers arrived at the station a few minutes before the arrival of the train, and arrested the station agent and put him under guard, then threw the train on the switch. The robbers were all large men, none of them under six feet tall. They were all masked and started in a southerly direction after they had robbed the train. They were all mounted on fine blooded horses. There is a hell of an excitement in this part of the country.

"[Signed] Ira A. Merrill."

Later information shows that Clell Miller and Arthur McCoy were members of the band, but there is still much dispute about the presence of Cole Younger, though the preponderance of evidence points to him as being one of the band.

# THE DEATH OF TWO DETECTIVES.

Plundering the train at Gad's Hill created an excitement never before equalled in eastern Missouri; armed bodies of men from nearly every point along the Iron Mountain road went out in pursuit of the marauders, stimulated to the greatest activity by large rewards offered by the railroad and express companies for the apprehension of the robbers. Several St. Louis detectives engaged in the search, and Pinkerton dispatched two of his best men to the haunts of the bandits. These officers were known as Capt. Allen, alias Lull, and James Wright, the latter having been in the Confederate service and claimed to be acquainted with the Younger boys. At Osceola, Missouri, the two detectives engaged the services of an ex-deputy sheriff named Edwin B. Daniels, and together the three penetrated the Monegaw Springs settlement, where the Youngers spent much of their time.

After leaving Osceola the official trio assumed the character of cattle dealers, and on March 16th, they set out on the road for Chalk Level, a little place about fifteen miles northwest of Osceola. On the route Lull and Daniels stopped at the farm-house of Theodore Snuffer, a distant relative of the Youngers, and asked for directions to widow Simms' house. Wright did not stop with his companions, but rode on, intending to spend a few moments with an acquaintance two miles west of Snuffer's.

By chance John and Jim Younger were stopping with Mr. Snuffer at the time, but did not show themselves. They listened intently, however, and after the directions were given as requested, they saw the detectives take a contrary road; this excited the suspicion of the two Youngers, and they decided to watch the strangers. For this purpose they mounted their horses and followed after Lull and Daniels for nearly a mile before coming up with them. The authentic particulars of this meeting are best given in the ante-mortem statement made by Capt. Allen, alias Lull, and subscribed to before justice of the peace St. Clair. It is as follows;

Yesterday, on the 16th of March, 1874, at about half past two o'clock p. m., E. B. Daniels and myself were riding along the road from Roscoe to Chalk Level, in. St. Clair county, which road leads past the house of one Theodore Snuffer. Daniels and myself were riding side by side, and our companion Wright was a short distance ahead of us; some noise behind us attracted our attention, and looking back we saw two men on horseback coming toward us; one was armed with a double-barrel shot-gun, the other with revolvers; don't know if the other had a shot-gun or not; the one that had the shot-gun carried it cocked, both barrels, and ordered us to halt; Wright drew his pistol but then put spurs to his horse and rode off; they ordered him to halt, and shot at him and shot off his hat, but he kept on riding. Daniels and myself stopped, standing across the road on our horses; they rode up to us, and ordered us to take off our pistols and drop them in the road, one of them covering me all the time with his gun. We dropped our pistols on the ground, and one of the men told the other to follow Wright and bring him back, but he refused to go, saying he would stay with him; one of the men then picked up the revolvers we had dropped, and looking at them, remarked they were damn fine pistols, and that we must make them a present of them; one of them asked me where we came from, and I said "Osceola;" he then wanted to know what we were doing in this part of the country; I replied, "Rambling around." One of them then said, "You were up here one day before." I replied that we were not. He then said we had been at the Springs. I replied that we had been at the Springs, but had not been inquiring for them, that we did not know them; they said detectives had been up there hunting for them all the time, and they were going to stop it. Daniels then said, "I am no detective; I can show you who I am and where I belong." And one of them said he knew him, and then turned to me and said, "What in the hell are you riding around here with all them pistols on for?" and I said, "Good God! is not every man wearing them that is traveling, and have I not as much right to wear them as any one else?" Then the one that had the shot-gun said, "Hold on, young man, we don't want any of that," and then lowered the gun, cocked, in a threatening manner. Then Daniels had some talk with them, and one of them got off his horse and picked up the pistols; two of them were mine and one was Daniels'; the one mounted had the gun drawn on me, and I concluded that they intended to kill us. I reached my hand behind me and drew a No. 2 Smith & Wesson pistol and cocked it and fired at the one on horseback; my horse became frightened at the report of the pistol and turned to run; then I heard two shots and my left arm fell; I had no control over my horse, and he jumped into the bushes before I could get hold of the rein with my right hand to bring him into the road; one of the men rode by and fired two shots at me, one of which took effect in my left side, and I lost all control of my horse again, and he turned into the brash, when a small tree struck me and knocked me out of the saddle. I then got up and staggered across the road and lay down until I was found. No one else was present.

W. J. ALLEN.

Subscribed and sworn to, before me, this 18th day of March, 1874.

JAMES ST. CLAIR.

The statement of Capt. Allen was used at the coroner's inquest over the bodies of Daniels and Younger, and the examining physicians gave the following testimony:

All we know concerning the death of the two men, being the same that the inquest is being held over, is that the one, John Younger, came to his death from the effects of a gun-shot wound, which entered the right side of his neck, touching the clavical bone, on the upper side, and about two inches from the meridian, went nearly straight through the neck; the orifice is small, indicating that he was shot with a small ball. The other man, Edwin B. Daniels, came to his death from the effect of a gunshot wound, which entered the left side of the neck, about one inch from the meridian line, and about midway of the neck, opposite the esophagus, and as per examination, went nearly straight through the neck, striking the bone; the orifice was pretty large, indicating that the ball was of a pretty large size.

A. C MARQUIS, M. D.

L. LEWIS, M. D.

Subscribed and sworn to before me, this 18th day of March, 1874.

JAMES ST. CLAIR, J. P.

The jury, with A. Ray as foreman, submitted a verdict to the effect that Daniels was killed by James Younger, and that John Younger met his death at the hands of W. J. Allen.

Capt. Allen was struck very hard in the left side, two inches above the hip; he was carried back to Roscoe, where he lingered for a period of six weeks, and then died, surrounded by his family that had come to him from Chicago directly after the shooting. His remains were enclosed in a metallic case and returned to Chicago, where they were buried with Masonic honors. Ed. Daniels was laid away in the little churchyard at Osceola, while John Younger sleeps under a neglected mound in old man Snuffer's orchard.

# ROBBING A TEXAS STAGE.

On the 7th of April, 1874, less than one month after the killing of John Younger, the stage running between Austin and San Antonio, Texas, was robbed under the following circumstances: On the day in question, the regular mail stage, carrying eleven passengers, was stopped by five masked bandits, at seven o'clock in the evening, twenty-three miles from Austin. They advanced to meet the stage and each of them presenting a heavy pistol, forced the stage-driver to halt, leave his seat and open the door of the vehicle. Among the passengers was Mr. Breckenridge, president of the First National Bank of San Antonio, who had. one thousand dollars on his person. Bishop Gregg, of the same city was also in the party, and three ladies, whose fright at seeing such a display of fire-arms, produced a panic inside the stage. The robbers were very courteous, but exacting, forcing an immediate compliance with their every request. All the passengers were made to get out and form in line, in the rear of the stage, where they were examined for money and valuables by two of the bandits, while the other three stood guard over their victims. The ladies, aside from the respectful language used toward them, were not partially treated by the outlaws, but, like their male companions, they were persuaded, by the peculiar means of the robbers, to give up all their money and watches. The total amount secured, including that gathered from the mail-bags, was about $3,000. Having appropriated all the valuables the passengers possessed, the bandits cut out the lead span of horses and taking these with them, they rode away rapidly toward the north.

The loss of two horses so delayed the stage that it was not until four o'clock on the following morning that it reached Austin; this prevented an early report of the robbery, so that fully eighteen hours had elapsed after the perpetration of the outrage, before the sheriff, with ten men, went in pursuit. The search for the robbers was fruitless for more than two weeks, the trail, seemingly, being thoroughly covered. After the sheriff returned home, a reward of $500 was offered for the capture of the bandits, and some time afterwards several detectives came upon a party by the name of Jim Reed, whom they suspected of having been one of the robbers, and in their efforts to arrest him, he fought his would-be captors until mortally wounded. Before dying, it is claimed, that he confessed to a participation in both the stage and Gad's Hill robberies. In the latter, it is said, his companions were Arthur McCoy and Jim Greenwood, but he refused to divulge the names of the two others.

It is more than probable, however, judging from later circumstances and confessions, that Jim Reed was not one of the stage robbers, and there is a prevailing suspicion that he never made any such confession as that attributed to him. There are hundreds who maintain that the robbers were Jesse and Frank James, Clell Miller, Cole Younger and Arthur McCoy. The facts, however, are involved in such a confusion of contradictory claims and statements that it is impossible to fix the robbery, positively, on any special persons.

The same stage was robbed again two years later in almost the identical spot and manner as in 1874, the robbers securing $2,000 and escaping without leaving any clue of their identity.

## COLE YOUNGER'S EPISTOLARY VINDICATION.

In the absence of positive testimony connecting the Younger brothers with all the robberies charged to them, and in order to avoid even a suspicion that intentional injustice is done them in this record of their lives, the writer, in a special correspondence with Cole Younger, asked him to make a written statement embodying his proofs and denials of any and all the crimes with which he and his brothers stand charged by current report, offering at the same time to publish it in full in this work. A very courteous reply was received, in which reference was made to a letter written by him to his brother-in-law Lycurgus Jones, of Cass county, and published in the Pleasant Hill Review, November 26th, 1874. It is but an act of justice that the letter be reproduced in this connection. It is as follows:

Cass County, November 15, 1874.

Dear Curg: — You may use this letter in your own way. I will give you this outline and sketch of my whereabouts and actions at the time of certain robberies with which I am charged. At the time of the Russellville bank robbery I was gathering cattle in Ellis county, Texas: cattle that I bought from Pleas Taylor and Rector. This can be proved by both of them; also by Sheriff Barkley and fifty other respectable men of that county. I brought the cattle to Kansas that fall and remained in St. Clair county until February. I then went to Arkansas and returned to St. Clair county about the first of May. I went to Kansas where our cattle were, in Woodson county, at Col. Ridge's. During the summer I was either in St. Clair, Jackson or Kansas, but as there was no robbery committed that summer, it makes no difference where I was.

The gate at the fair grounds at Kansas City was robbed that fall. I was in Jackson county at the time. I left R. P. Rose's that morning, went down the Independence road, stopped at Dr. Noland's and got some pills. Brother John was with me. I went through Independence, and from there to Ace Webb's. There I took dinner and then went to Dr. L. W. Twiman's. Staid there until after supper, then went to Silas Hudspeth's and stayed all night. This was the day the gate was robbed at Kansas City. Next day John and I went to Kansas City. We crossed the river at Blue Mills, and went upon the other side. Our business there was to see E. P. West. He was not at home, but the family will remember that we were there. We crossed on the bridge, stayed in the city all night, and the next morning we rode up through the city. I met several of my friends, among them was Bob Hudspeth. We then returned to the Six-Mile country by the way of Independence. At Big Blue we met Jas. Chiles and had a long talk with him. I saw several friends that were standing at or near the gate, and they all said they didn't know any of the party that did the robbing. Neither John nor I was accused of the crime for several days after. My name would never have been used in connection with the affair, had not Jesse W. James, for some cause, best known to himself, published in the Kansas City Times, a letter stating that John, myself and he were accused of the robbery. Where he got his authority I don't know, but one thing I do know, he had none from me. We were not on good terms at the time, nor haven't been for several years. From that time on mine and John's names have been connected with the James brothers. John hadn't seen either of them for eighteen months before his death. And as for A. C. McCoy, John never saw him in his life. I knew A. C. McCoy during the war, but haven't seen him since, notwithstanding the Appleton City paper says he has been with us in that county for two years. Now, if any respectable man in that county will say he ever saw A. C. McCoy with me or John, I will say no more; or if any respectable man will say that he ever saw any one with us who suited the description of A. C. McCoy, then I will be silent and never more plead innocence.

McCoy is forty-eight or forty-nine years old; six feet and over high; dark hair and blue eyes, and low forehead.

Poor John, he has been hunted down and shot like a wild beast, and never was a boy more innocent. But there is a day coming when the secrets of all hearts will be laid open before that All-seeing eye, and every act of our lives will be scrutinized, then will his skirts be white as the driven snow, while those of his accusers will be doubly dark.

I will now come to the Ste. Genevieve robbery. At that time I was in St. Clair county, Missouri. I do not remember the date, but Mr. Murphy, one of our neighbors, was sick about that time, and I sat up with him regularly, where I met with some of the neighbors every day. Dr. L. Lewis was his physician.

As to the Iowa train robbery, I have forgotten the day, I was also in St. Clair county, Missouri, at that time, and had the pleasure of attending preaching the evening previous to the robbery, at Monegaw Springs. There were fifty or a hundred persons there who will testify in any court that I and John were there. I will give you the names of some of them: Simeon C. Bruce, John S. Wilson, James Van-Allen, Rev. Mr. Smith and lady. Helvin Fickle and lady of Greenton Valley, were attending the Springs at that time, and either of them will testify to the above, for John and I sat in front of Mr. Smith while he was preaching, and had the pleasure of his company for a few moments, together with his lady, and Mr. and Mrs. Fickle, after service. They live at Greenton Valley, Lafayette county, Missouri, and their evidence would be taken in the Court of Heaven. As there was no other robbery committed until January, I will come to that time. About the last of December, 1873, I arrived in Carroll parish, Louisiana. I stayed there until the 8th of February, 1874. I and brother stayed at Wm. Dickerson's, near Floyd, Dickerson was Master of a Masonic lodge, and during the time the Shreveport stage and the Hot Springs stage were robbed; also the Gad's Hill robbery. Now, if the Governor or any one else wants to satisfy himself in regard to the above, he can write to the Masonic Fraternity, Floyd, Carroll parish, Louisiana. I hope the leading journals will investigate the matter, and then, if they find I have misrepresented anything, they can show me up to the world as being guilty, but if they find it as I have stated, they surely would have no objections to state the facts as they are.

You can appeal to the Governor in your own language, and if he will send men to investigate the above, and is not satisfied of my innocence, then he can offer the reward for Thos. Coleman Younger, and if he finds me to be innocent, he can make a statement to that effect. I write this hurriedly, and I suppose I have given outlines enough. I want you to take pains and write a long letter for me and sign my name in full.

THOMAS COLEMAN YOUNGER.

# THE TRAIN ROBBERY AT MUNCIE, KANS.

Remaining in Texas until late in the fall, the outlaws finding no special divertisement or opportunity to enrich themselves, decided to return north and put into operation plans for robberies which would yield large results. Through their communications with one another and, especially, it would appear, with accomplices in the extreme West, it was learned that a large amount of money and gold dust would be shipped from Denver to the east, via the Kansas Pacific Railroad, on the 12th of December following. A scheme was at once devised for the interception and appropriation of the treasure. To accomplish this design, the band, consisting of Cole and Bob Younger, Jesse and Frank James, and Clell Miller, took into their confidence a worthless fellow in Kansas City, named Bud McDaniels. There is another story to the effect that McDaniels had learned of the intended valuable shipment through a friend in Denver, and that, communicating this knowledge to the bandits named, the six then confederated together, with pledges of confidence, to accomplish the robbery.

On the 13th of December, the outlaws, being well mounted, left Jackson county without the discovery having been made of their presence in the locality, and rode over to Wyandotte county. The localities along the railroad were inspected for the purpose of selecting the most available place for the successful perpetration of the crime then in contemplation. The spot finally chosen was one mile east of Muncie, Kansas, and five miles west of Kansas City. This selection was made because there was a water-tank at the place at which trains almost invariably stopped, and because the Kaw river ran alongside the road, with a margin of heavy timber and brush, in which the bandits secreted themselves, after placing a pile of old ties on the track, to await the train which was due at 4:45 in the afternoon. They had been under cover only a short time, when a bank of smoke in the distance and the singing sound that ran along the rails, signalled the approaching train. It happened, on that particular occasion, the engine did not require water and would have run by had not the engineer discovered a pile of ties on the track, which compelled a stop. At the moment the train came to a stand-still, the robbers sprang from out their hiding-place and advancing with menacing weapons, forced a compliance with their demands. Each one of the bandits was thoroughly masked and their appearance indicated determination. One of these, since believed to have been McDaniels, covered the engineer and fireman with his pistols, while the others distributed themselves among the passengers and the express car. They uncoupled and made the engineer pull the express car forward about one hundred feet, when they forced the messenger to open the safe, and took about $30,000 in currency and $25,000 worth of gold dust. They also robbed some of the passengers of money, but left them their watches. There was some jewelry in the express car which the thieves took, however, and this furnished the evidence which gave them away in a short time. The horses of the gang were hitched in a little clump of brush in plain sight of the train, and after they had done, the passengers saw them run across the intervening open ground and mount their horses with the sack full of plunder. They rode away and crossed the Kaw river bridge, passing within five miles of Kansas City. Late that evening they overtook a man named Steele and made him exchange horses with one of them.

After the train reached Kansas City due report was made of the robbery and an armed band of about twenty-five persons went in pursuit. The track was easily found and on the day following, the sheriff's posse traced the bandits through Westport, Jackson county, and discovered the spot, five miles south-east of that place, where they had camped, and doubtless divided their booty.

The robbers made directly for their secret haunts on the Blue, however, and further search by the authorities proved unavailing.

The old band of outlaws was immediately charged with the crime, chiefly because of the manner in which the robbery was completed; the well-known, distinguishing marks of the bandits so familiar with that section, afforded almost conclusive evidence, though the circumstantial testimony would never have been sufficient for the conviction of any of the old band, had they been arrested.

Two days after the robbery Bud McDaniels hired a horse and buggy in Kansas City for the purpose of treating his girl to a ride. Proceeding to her house, he found she was absent, and being much provoked, he drank frequently and was soon driving through the streets in a very reckless manner, indicative of a decidedly drunken condition. He was at length arrested by the police, and on searching him at the station-house preparatory to locking him up to sober off, they found on him $1,034 in money, two revolvers and some jewelry, which he said he had bought to give his girl. His statement as to where he bought it was not very definite, and, besides, the description of the jewelry taken from the train had been furnished to the police. Suspicion was instantly aroused, and investigation resulted in the positive identification of the jewelry. It was also found that Bud had been out of town. The case was too clear. He had to go back to Kansas to stand his trial. He had a preliminary examination and was held to answer before the grand-jury. He had refused to breathe a word about his confederates.

McDaniels was confined for a considerable time in the Lawrence jail; when he was taken out by a deputy sheriff, who attempted to conduct him to the court-house for trial; McDaniels made a break and succeeded in escaping. After enjoying his liberty for about one week, he was discovered, and in the effort to again arrest him, the officers, meeting with resistance, one of them shot him dead.

# THE HUNTINGTON, VIRGINIA, BANK ROBBERY.

After the train robbery there was a short separation of the outlaws, some going to Texas and others proceeding east, where identification was less liable, for the purpose of enjoying the sights of New York and Washington. Each of the band was now provided with sufficient wealth to dissipate every desire, for the time, except the best and most enjoyable means for spending it.

During a short residence in the East, Cole Younger formed the acquaintance of a sharp, black-eyed fellow who went by the name of Jack Keen, alias Tom Webb. This man had spent many years in Kentucky and West Virginia, being at all times a suspicious character, and it was he who proposed the robbery of the bank at Huntington. Cole Younger and Frank James considered the proposition, and meeting Tom, or Tomlinson McDaniels, a brother of Bud's, at Petersburgh, they laid the scheme before him, and then the four concluded to raid the bank.

The plan for the robbery being perfected, the bandits decided to wait until fall, when the bank would probably carry a large amount of money for the handling of the harvests.

On the first of September, 1875, the well armed and mounted quartette rode into Huntington, each wearing a long linen ulsterette over a heavy fall coat. They made directly for the bank, where two of them dismounted, leaving the other pair on horseback to clear the streets of people. The latter two then opened a fusillade with their pistols, driving every one indoors, while their companions entered the bank, and with presented pistols forced the cashier, R. T. Oney, to open the vault. One of the bandits kept his pistol pointed at the cashier and a citizen, who chanced to be in the bank at the time, to prevent an outcry, while the other searched the safe and drawers carefully, from which he gathered about ten thousand dollars. Having secured all the funds of the bank, the two ran out and gave a shrill whistle. The others responded quickly, bringing up the two horses for the dismounted bandits. Then succeeded the clatter of fast speeding horses' feet as the outlaws dashed out of town, to be pursued a few hours afterward by twenty resolute men, while telegrams were sent in every direction for the interception of the robbers. The pursuit then began with remarkable earnestness, posses of armed citizens joining in the chase from every direction. The outlaws had frequent fights with their pursuers, and were several times forced to abandon their horses and take to the brush on foot. They kept working southwest through the mountains. Occasionally they would steal horses and make a forced march, but the whole country was aroused and out against them. Daily reports from the pursuers were sent in every direction, showing just where the bandits were last seen, and which way they were going, calling on the people to look out for them, etc. And the people turned out. After ten days of incessant ambuscade, one of them met his fate at Pine Hill, Kentucky. There were two brothers named Dillon, who, becoming very much interested in the reports concerning the bandits, concluded that from the route given that the robbers would come near their place. Each of them pro- cured an old army musket which they loaded with slugs, and then kept a sharp lookout for the outlaws. On the night of the 14th, which was cloudless, and with a new moon which rendered objects visible, the two brothers in maintaining their watch saw four figures moving through the woods on foot about fifty yards south of them. When the outlaws approached the road they stopped, and consulting together for a moment, they separated, two of them proceeding down the road, while the other pair came directly toward the brothers. Now was the supreme moment. The watchers could not be mistaken; two tall men wearing linen dusters and with pistols, the handles of which protruded from the front of their coats. Two to two without any odds provided the first fire could be made effectual. But what if those two muskets should fail fire, or, firing, miss? The Dillon boys perhaps never thought of this; like the enthusiastic hunter who attacks a grizzly bear, he only thinks of the game before him; evidently the brothers were prompted by a similar enthusiasm, for as the two bandits approached the brothers commanded a "halt! throw up your arms." Instead of obeying the injunction, the bandits drew their pistols and four shots were fired; each one giving an exchange. After the firing the outlaws ran off, one of them moving in a manner that indicated suffering.

On the following morning the two brothers visited the spot where the engagement had occurred, and made an examination; they were rewarded by finding blood stains on the leaves, and following the trail into a cornfield for a distance of two hundred yards, they found a man with a gaping wound in his side, within hand-reach of death's threshold. The brothers tenderly carried him up to their home, and laying the tortured body upon the bed, sent quickly for a surgeon. The wounded bandit, with the fever and damp of dissolution on his brow, cried out in his delirium for "Bud," and then in the last moments, as the hand of death, lifting the veil of unconsciousness like one who draws the drapery from the face of the dead, for a last look, the robber exclaimed, "Yes, I'm dying, where are my friends?"

The question was asked him, "What is your name, and who were your companions?"

Looking sternly into the face of the questioner, he replied, in a gurgling whisper: "Did you think approaching death would make me a coward? I never betrayed a friend."

The eyes did not close, but continued their withering stare until a film grew o'er the sight; until those around the bed-side looked down into the shallow depths of a dead man's eyes.

On the body of the outlaw there was found only a seal ring and two photographs; one of a man who proved to be Bob Ricketts, who said Tom McDaniels was the only person who had his picture; and the other of a woman who was recognized as an old sweetheart of McDaniels. The same woman received, some days afterward, a piece of black crape enclosed in a letter. The seal ring was identified as one McDaniels had worn.

On the day succeeding the robber's death, September 19th, three men came to the house where the body lay and asked the privilege of viewing the remains. It so happened that only Mrs. Dillon and some lady friends were present at the time, who became frightened, correctly suspicioning that the three were the surviving bandits of the Huntington raid. Mrs. Dillon, therefore, refused the request by saying that the remains were in the coffin which had already been permanently closed. There was a sign of disappointment on the faces of the men for a moment, but the largest one directly spoke in a firm tone of voice, saying:

"Madam, we are sorry that circumstances require us to appear rude; we came to see the dead body. and therefore ask you again, this time firmly, to show us the remains."

Mrs. Dillon, somewhat frightened before, immediately conducted the three strangers into another room where the coffin rested on two chairs. A screw-driver lay on the window-casing, and with this the lid was readily removed, which, being turned aside was held by Mrs. Dillon while the trio looked long and sorrowfully at the pale, upturned face of the dead man. The largest man betrayed great emotion, the tears straggling down his cheeks and falling on the cerements of his comrade. Standing there and looking down into the sightless, but opened eyes of the dead robber, who can conceive the reflections of the surviving bandits who had lured the poor unfortunate to that wicket of life from out which no soul can ever come to tell its story.

After a speechless gaze of many minutes, with manifestations of deep sorrow, the three men asked if the party who did the killing was about; being informed that he was not, they courteously bade Mrs. Dillon good-day and departed, going out through the corn-field.

Mr. Oney, the Huntington cashier, had been to Pine Hill, the second day before this occurrence, and had fully identified the wounded man as one of the two who entered the bank and made him give up the money. He returned by way of Louisville, and, while there, received the following dispatch, which was published in the Courier-Journal:

Louisville, Ky., Sept. 20.

Robt. T. Oney: — The other three entered the house and had the coffin opened; said he did not look like he did before. One of them was crying. They asked for me and then went into the corn-field. I was at the house about five minutes after they left. I look for a desperate attack to-day.

W. R. Dillon.

There was no attack of course. The three survivors bushwhacked about for some time, two of them eventually escaping, while the third was wounded and captured in Fentress county, Tennessee. He had about him some $4,000 in money. He was identified as one of the men who wore a long duster at Huntington, and was taken back and given twelve years in Moundsville prison. He was booked Jack Kean, alias Tom Webb.

In justice to Cole Younger and Frank James, the following suspicions concerning the identity of the other two robbers are given; for the intention of the writer is to draw no inference not supported by reasonable conclusions. Regardless of the information which led to introducing Cole Younger and Frank James as plotting with Jack Kean the robbery of the bank, the evidence is not convincing that either of them were at Huntington. It is claimed that Clell Miller was one of the party, while the fourth man is in dispute. Some hold that it was Cole Younger, because Cole was commonly called "Bud" by his comrades, and they think Thomp. McDaniels' delirious inquiries as to whether Bud was captured, referred to Cole or "Bud" Younger. Others say that McDaniels, being out of his head, was thinking and raving about his brother Bud. The matter was never settled. The following is a description of the robbers, published a few days after the raid:

No. 1. Heavy-set man, at least six feet high, weight two hundred pounds, tolerably dark hair, with reddish whiskers and moustache, red complexion, black hat, long linen duster and blue overalls, gold ring on left little finger.

No. 2. Tall, slim man, in height about six feet, one hundred and fifty pounds, delicate-looking, light hair and sandy whiskers, high forehead, long nose, gold buttons in shirt, left little finger had a ring, long duster and blue overalls.

No. 3. Tall, slim man, about six feet high, weight one hundred and sixty-five pounds, short, black whiskers and black hair, slim face, black hat, long duster, blue overalls, suit of black twilled cloth with stripes, fine boots, two gold rings on little left finger; had two collars washed with "London" printed on the bands.

No. 4, Heavy-set man, about five feet ten inches high, weight one hundred and eighty pounds, very stout, square-looking man, brown hair, round red face, patch of red whiskers on his chin, light-colored hat, linen duster, gray striped coat and vest, pants similar, but not like coat and vest, red drilling overalls, fine boots, broad gold ring with flowers cut in it on his left little finger.

It should have been stated that while in the bank one of the robbers dropped a small jewelry ornament, on one side of which was engraved the name "A. S. Underwood" and from this and the direction of the flight, it was thought some of the Kentucky Underwoods might have been in the band. This appears to have had little weight, however, with the authorities. On the 11th of March, 1876, a man named Keeney was arrested at Sedalia, Mo., on suspicion of having had some hand in the Huntington raid. He was a poor man, and was found to have received a large sum of money by express from a brother living near Huntington. He gave no explanation satisfactory to the authorities, but in the absence of any positive evidence, even tending to show his connection with the robbery, he was released after a confinement of two weeks.

# THE MISSOURI PACIFIC RAILROAD ROBBERY.

More than one year elapsed after the robbery at Huntington before the bandits were heard of again. In this interim of activity the Younger and James brothers were in Texas and Indian Territory, with old friends and war comrades. A few detectives were still on the search, but only as an auxiliary to other work, there being no prospect of arresting either of the outlaws.

The policy of the bandits was to conceal their presence, even from friends, just before perpetrating a robbery, so as to make the crime such a thorough surprise, that after its commission people would be too badly confused for an immediate and intelligent pursuit.

The old tactics of the outlaws were put into practice at the Missouri Pacific Railroad robbery, one of the most daring and successful sorties ever made by the "Knights of the Rail." The particulars of this bold adventure are as follows:

About 9 o'clock on the night of the 7th of July, 1876, Henry Chateau, the old Swiss watchman, at the Otter bridge on the Missouri Pacific Railroad, was sitting by the pump-house smoking his cob-pipe and enjoying the balmy air of the evening. The sound of voices fell on his ear, and looking out into the shadow he saw four men walking across the bridge toward him. It was an isolated, out-of-the-way place, and though strangers did not very often pass, their very scarcity made company the more welcome. The men came along and proved to be right sociable fellows. Three of them sat down, passed the compliments of the evening, and talked a few minutes about anything that occurred to mind. Presently the fourth, who was a tremendously big fellow, standing just in front of the watchman, asked, "What kind of a job have you got? What do you have to do here? "

"Just watch the bridge," was the reply. "If there is danger I show the red light and the train stops. If all is safe I show the white light and she goes on."

The big fellow remarked that that was a good easy job. Then turning to one of his comrades he asked,

"What time is it?"

"Ten minutes after nine," said the other.

"It's about time."

One of the others rose to his feet and asked for a drink of water. The watchman stepped into the pump-house to get it, and was suddenly seized. A revolver was placed at his head and he was a prisoner. The next thing he discovered was that all the men had pulled out masks and slipped them on. The large man then said:

"Come, follow us, and be quiet."

Trembling with fear the watchman pleadingly inquired:

"You do not intend to kill me?"

"What do we want to kill you for?" replied the leader, "we only want you to do what you're told, and if you are wise you'll do It without any questions."

The large fellow then pulled from his pocket a handkerchief, with which the prisoner was blindfolded, and then taking up the white and red lights, the parties crossed the bridge and walked for more than a mile along the track, when they came to a deep rocky cut, two miles east of Otterville, where the captive watchman was ordered to be seated, two of the robbers maintaining guard over him. Meantime others of the gang heaped a lot of ties on the track.

Presently the train was heard in the distance. Then one of the bandits lighted the red lantern which he placed in the watchman's hand and led him out on the track, telling him to stand there and stop the train or be run over, or shot, just as he chose. The train consisted of two baggage, one express, three passenger and two sleeping-cars, John Standthorpe engineer, and Capt. Tebbitts conductor. On came the train, and the prisoner, who conceived death staring him from every side, made industrious use of the signal. The vigilant engineer saw it, and applying the air-brakes brought the locomotive to a standstill about twenty feet from the frightened watchman. Pistol shots were heard, and the old man slightly moving the bandage over his eyes, saw that his guards had vanished; frightened, then, at what he could not define, the watchman threw down the lantern and fled through the woods in the darkness.

The cow-catcher of the engine had actually pushed in amongst the pile of ties on the track, and had the train stopped less promptly, the engine would have been ditched.

The engineer and fireman had company in an instant. Two masked men shoved revolvers at them, telling them to take it easy and come along. They were quickly escorted to the baggage car and forced in. Others of the band had instantly piled an obstruction on the track behind the train so that it could not back out, and also dispatched a man to the bridge to flag a freight-train shortly due. Still others at the sides of the train kept the passengers indoors, firing and warning all not to come out.

The work of robbing was executed with a coolness unparalleled in the history of crimes of this kind. The express messenger, J. B. Bushnell, had in his charge a through safe of the Adams Express Company, for which he had no key, and a United States Express safe. The messenger, divining what was up as soon as the train stopped, made his way back to one of the sleepers and gave the United States safe key to a brakeman, who put it in his shoe; hence, when three of the robbers rushed into the express car, which was also a baggage car, they found the baggageman sitting there looking demure. They asked him for keys to the safes, and when he said he had none they searched him. Then they advised him somewhat earnestly to hunt them up or say his prayers. Finally he convinced them that he was not the messenger. Without a moment's warning they bade him show them the messenger. Through the train they marched him in front of their revolvers until the messenger was found. The arguments used to induce him to give up the key proved irresistible. The brakeman was pointed out, the shoe pulled off and the key found, the messenger and brakeman were then marched forward to the baggage car and locked in, with the injunction not to be "too fly." The United States safe contents were speedily transferred to a grain sack without examination. The messenger once more found himself in peril, because he had no key to the Adams through safe, but as his explanation was reasonable, the robbers were convinced. One of the bandits then ran out, got the fireman's hammer and began banging at the safe. He was unable to produce much impression, whereupon a herculean bandit caught the hammer and with a few tremendous blows broke a hole in the side, into which he vainly attempted to force his hand. The first striker, however, remarked that he "wore a No. 7 kid," and could do better. In just two minutes the safe was plundered and the booty bagged. No attempt was made to rob the passengers. The train-boy's box was broken open, and peanuts and apples were gobbled up voraciously. Only one or two shots were fired from the train, the robbers keeping up a fusillade on both sides and moving from point to point, so that in the darkness it seemed as though the brush was full of men.

The train-boy had a revolver, and early in the fracas he stepped out on the platform and blazed away at one of the robbers, who gave a loud croaking laugh and called out, "Hear that little — bark!"

As soon as the safes had been emptied, the robbers told the train-men to remove the obstructions before and behind and pull out, which was done with alacrity. The train was stopped an hour and ten minutes, and the booty secured amounted to fifteen thousand dollars.

All the robbers who were seen in the cars were tall men, except the one who said he wore the No. 7 kid, and he was the only one who wore no mask. The others were masked in various ways, some having the whole face covered, except holes for the eyes, and some having a mask covering only the nose and lower part of the face. The one who seemed to be the leader was tall and had light or yellowish hair.

The mustering for the pursuit was hot and zealous. Bacon Montgomery started out from Sedalia with a picked crowd and ran the robbers to within three miles of Florence, where they scattered temporarily and took to the hills. Sheriff Murray led another band. On every side the country was in arms. The robbers were eight in number. It was found where they had eaten at farm houses the day before the robbery. Accurate descriptions were given, and it was positively stated that the Youngers had been recognized both on the advance and retreat. Maj. Wood accordingly visited the Younger settlement and reported that the boys had not been away from home. The Osage river was high, all the fords were guarded, and from the other side the country was scouted over in every direction, yet the robbers were cunning enough to get away without apparently ever being run to close quarters. Matters fell to a dead quiet, and the pursuit changed to a still hunt, till about the first of August, when Hobbs Kerry and Bruce Younger were arrested at Joplin and Granby, the St. Louis police having taken a hand at working up the case. Bruce Younger was soon discharged, as it was easily shown that he was not at Otterville. Kerry, however, was positively identified. It appears the name of every member of the band had been definitely ascertained, and most of them had been traced to their lairs. Charley Pitts and Bill Chadwell had gone to Cherokee and Coalfield, Kansas, where an attempt was made to arrest them by agreement on the same day Kerry was taken in. Pitts was captured on Spring river with one thousand eight hundred dollars in his pocket, but subsequently got away. He had been engaged to marry a widow named Lillie Beamer, but about three weeks after the robbery he married another girl in Coalfield. As he had already temporarily intrusted a two thousand dollar package to Mrs. Beamer, and talked freely about the robbery, she was not slow to tell of it when he married the other girl. Pitts' real name was Wells. An effort was made to arrest Chadwell the same time that Pitts was taken, but he got into a cornfield and escaped. The officers, who were sheriff's deputies, then rushed back into Missouri after the James and Younger Boys, but as usual did not get them. Kerry made a full confession about a week after he was captured. He said Cole and Bob Younger, Frank and Jesse James, Clell Miller, Charles Pitts, Bill Chadwell and himself did the job. They rode twenty miles the first night before dividing the money. Then they emptied the sack, ripped open the packages, put all the money in a pile and Frank James counted it. Kerry's duty was to watch the horses while the robbery was being accomplished. His share was one thousand two hundred dollars. Then he and Chadwell and Pitts went out together. They got away easy enough. Kerry left them and went to Vinita, then back to Granby, where he spent money, gambled, gave himself away and was sent to the penitentiary for four years. The usual proffer of an alibi came from the James Boys in spite of Kerry and the widow Beamer.

# THE NORTHFIELD BANK ROBBERY AND TRAGEDY, CAPTURE OF THE YOUNGER BROTHERS.

The Rocky Cut, or Missouri Pacific Railroad robbery, caused a separation of the bandits for only a brief period. Jesse and Frank James, with Charlie Pitts, Clell Miller and Bill Chadwell, went directly to Texas, finding a safe retreat in the western part of that State. The Younger Brothers proceeded to Jackson county and withdrew into the secret cavern, where they felt secure against molestation. From time to time, however, they visited reliable friends in the adjoining counties, but were extremely careful to escape the observation of strangers.

About the middle of August Cole Younger concluded to visit Texas, and in order to make the trip without interference, he conceived the idea of masking his identity behind the make-up of a teamster. To prepare for the journey, he went to Lees Summit, accompanied by his brothers, Jim and Bob, where, after a short stay, he purchased a pair of horses and a substantial wagon, which being loaded with provisions of various kinds, the three started for Texas on the following day. They had proceeded only a few miles in Kansas, through which the route was taken, when they met the James Brothers with their confederates, Clell Miller, Charley Pitts and Bill Chadwell. How this meeting occurred, whether by accident or in pursuance of arrangements perfected through correspondence, the writer cannot say, but the natural conclusion would be that it was intentional. At this meeting plans were discussed respecting the plundering of a bank in Minnesota.

Bill Chadwell, alias Styles, who was with the James Boys, had been a former resident of Minnesota, in which State he had some respectable relations. His acquaintance in the eastern part of the State led to a consideration of the results of a bank robbery in that section. He told a long and plausible story concerning the wealth of that country; the heavy deposits carried by some of the banks, that of Mankato being especially mentioned, and then declared his knowledge of every road and hog path, cave and swamp within two hundred miles of St. Paul. His story produced a most favorable impression upon the two James boys and Clell Miller, who, in turn, sought to persuade Cole Younger and his brothers into a similar disposition. It is said that Jim and Bob Younger thought favorable of the enterprise, but Cole shook his head and expressed doubts and dissatisfaction. He plainly told his comrades that Minnesota was too far from home for a successful adventure of the character proposed, and that "the game was not worth the ammunition." However, the will of all the others prevailed against his good judgment, and selling his team and provisions, the reorganized party proceeded to Minnesota by railroad.

After reaching the section of their intended exploit, it was decided to make Chadwell the leader, because of his knowledge of the country. In accordance with his suggestions the bandits separated into pairs, coming together again, as occasion required, in order to preserve a concert of action. In riding through the country they went sometimes in pairs and then again there were three in one company and five in another, carrying with them county and section maps, that their retreat might be made with a thorough understanding of all the avenues affording the best means of escape. At some places they claimed to be railroad surveyors, which was their excuse for making inquiries regarding swamps, bluffs and stretches of heavy timber. At other times, in crossing prairies, they passed for land speculators and cattle dealers.

It is positively known now that the bandits visited the cities of Minneapolis, St. Paul, Mankato, Jaynesville. Lake Crystal, Owatonna, Dundas, Madelia and Northfield, and in each of these places they stopped at the hotels and demeaned themselves like wealthy gentlemen. They purchased horses at different points until all the bandits were superbly mounted.

At Mankato all the outlaws came together on the 3d of September, and paid a visit to the city bank, where one of them obtained change for a $50 bill. During their stay in this place Jesse James was recognized by an old acquaintance, but the recognition was not returned, Jesse claiming that the speaker was a stranger. After this only five of the bandits were seen together until the attack at Northfield; the reason for this is found in the arrangement for Bill Chadwell and Cole Younger 'to ride in advance and obtain necessary information which would determine the party upon what bank the raid should be made. When the bandits rode into Mankato on the 5th of September, they all wore long, linen ulsterettes over their heavy coats. On Wednesday, the 6th of September, 1876, three rode in from Millersburg and met a fourth. All tied their horses near the depot, where they were admired by fanciers of fine stock. Two weeks before the raid two of them had purchased horses in St. Paul, and Officer Kenny recognized one of them as Clell Miller, whom he had seen on trial at Corydon, Iowa, for the bank robbery committed there in 1871. Miller talked with the officer, whom he also recognized. He said he was going to the Black Hills. All the gang appear to have obtained a good knowledge of the town and immediate vicinity without exciting suspicion that they were other than honest cattle dealers with plenty of money.

On the following day, the 7th, the eight daring brigands rode into Northfield, a town of two thousand inhabitants, located on the line of the Milwaukee and St. Paul Railroad, in Rice county. A small stream runs through the place, called Cannon river, over which there is a neat iron bridge, and just above this there is an excellent mill race, with a large flouring mill owned by Messrs. Ames & Co. The town is chiefly noted for the location of Carlton College, one of the finest educational institutions in the State.

Just before noon three of the bandits dined at Jeft's restaurant on the west side of Cannon river. After eating they talked politics, and one of them offered to bet the restaurant man one hundred dollars that the State would go Democratic. The bet was not taken, and they then rode across the bridge into the business part of the town, hitching their horses nearly in front of the First National Bank. They stood for some time talking leisurely near the corner. Suddenly there came like a whirlwind a rush of horsemen over the bridge. There were only three of them, but they made racket enough for a regiment. Riding into the square with whoops and oaths, they began firing revolvers and ordering everybody off the streets. Almost at the same moment two others rode down from the west, carrying out a similar programme. It was a new experience for Northfield, and for a few minutes the slamming of front doors almost drowned the noise of the firing. At the first sound of the onset the three men who first entered town, Jesse James, Charley Pitts and Bob Younger, had walked quickly into the bank and leaped nimbly over the counter. The cashier, J. L. Haywood, was at his place and Frank Wilcox and A. E. Bunker, clerks, were at their desks. All were covered by the revolvers before they apprehended danger. The robbers stated that they intended to rob the bank. The cashier was commanded to open the safe, and bravely refused. The outer door of the vault was standing ajar, and the leader stepped in to try the inner door. As he did so Haywood jumped forward and tried to shut him in. One of the others, afterward found to be Charlie Pitts, promptly arrested the movement. At this moment Bunker thought he saw a chance, and so he broke for the back door. The third robber, Bob Younger, followed and fired two shots, one of which took effect in the fugitive's shoulder. The others then insisted that Haywood should open the safe, and putting a knife to his throat said, "Open up, d — d you, or we'll slit you from ear to ear." A slight cut was made to enforce the demand. Haywood still refused. Meantime the firing outside had commenced, and the men then began to cry out, "Hurry up! It's getting too hot here!" The three hastily ransacked the drawers, and finding only a lot of small change, jumped over the railing and ran out. Jesse James was the last to go, and as he was in the act of leaping from the counter, he saw Haywood turn quickly to a drawer as if in the act of securing a weapon. Instantly the outlaw presented his pistol and shot the brave cashier dead. The bullet penetrated the right temple and ranging downward lodged near the base of the brain. Haywood fell over without a groan, a quantity of his blood and brains staining the desk as he reeled in the death fall. The shot which struck Bunker entered his right shoulder at the point of the shoulder-blade and passed through obliquely, producing only a flesh wound.

As the bandits rushed into the street they met a sight and reception quite unexpected. Recovering from their first surprise, the citizens began to exhibit their pluck, and were ready to meet the outlaws half way in a deadly fight. A search for fire-arms was the first important step, and Dr. Wheeler, J. B. Hide, L. Stacey, Mr. Manning and Mr. Bates each succeeded in procuring a weapon which they expeditiously put into service. Dr. Wheeler, from a corner room (No. 8) in the Dampier House, with a breech-loading carbine, took deliberate aim at one of the bandits as he was mounting, and sent a big slug through the outlaw's body. The death-stricken man plunged head-long from his horse and never uttered a sound afterward. This man proved to be Bill Chadwell, or properly Bill Styles.

Mr. Bates was in a room over Hananer's clothing-store in the Scriver block, while Manning stood fearlessly on the sidewalk, and the two kept firing at the robbers as opportunity presented. At length Manning walked out, and seeing one of the bandits riding rapidly up Division street, he fired and was rewarded by seeing the robber grow unsteady in his seat, and then checking the speed of his horse, tumble to the ground. This second victim proved to be Clell Miller, and as he fell, Cole Younger, seeing the fatal result, rode up to the prostrate comrade from whose body he unbuckled a belt containing two pistols, securing which, he remounted and rode back to the others who were still firing. Another of the outlaws used his horse as a barricade, and from behind it he continued to shoot until another shot from Manning's gun killed the animal. His protection being destroyed the bandit ran for the iron stairway which leads to the second story of the Scriver block from the outside. Behind this stairway were a number of empty pine boxes, from behind which the bandit used every effort to kill Manning. Dr. Wheeler was a critical observer of everything occurring in the street, and bringing his carbine to bear on the outlaw, he fired, sending a bullet through the bandit's right elbow. This man proved to be Bob Younger, who, not in the least discouraged by his painful wound, coolly maintained his position, and, shifting his pistol to the left hand, fired at Bates, who was standing with his weapon upraised inside his store. The bullet sped through a window plate and cut a furrow through Mr. Bates' cheek, but not deep enough to draw much blood.

A Norwegian by the name of Nicholas Gustavason, was on the street, when one of the bandits ordered him to get indoors. His limited knowledge of the English language caused his death, for not understanding the command the outlaw shot him in the head, producing a wound from which he died four days afterward.

By some means Jim Younger lost his horse, and the other bandits, finding the citizens' fire too destructive, mounted their horses and fled. At this moment Jim shouted, "My God! boys, you don't intend to desert me? I am shot!" At this Cole Younger dashed back and took his wounded brother up behind him. The gang then rode rapidly out of town, going in a westwardly direction.

After getting out of Northfield the outlaws galloped hard for a mile, and then stopped for a few minutes to dress their hurts. It was afterward ascertained that every man in the party was wounded more or less severely, some of them being merely punctured with small shot. This was the result of Mr. Stacy's double-barrel shot-gun, which he had no time to charge with large shot. At Dundas, three miles from Northfield, they stopped again and made another application of cold water and bandages. One of them was so badly hurt that another of the band got on the horse with him to hold him on, the riderless horse being led by a comrade. Thus adjusted the six rode away again. On the road they met a man by the name of Empey, hauling a load of hoop-poles. As he had one fine horse they knocked him into the ditch, cut the horses out of the harness and went ahead a little way, when they had to pull up again to dress their wounds. Starting on again they stopped another farmer, but concluding that his horses were not as good as some of their wounded ones, let him go. At this time Frank James was wearing a bandage around his leg outside his trousers, and Jim Younger had a cloth around his arm and was holding one hand in the other, the blood dripping from his fingers, while his horse was led by a comrade. This, of course, explains how it happened that they got away no faster. Had they abandoned the worst wounded ones to their fate, there is little doubt but that the others would have gotten away easily enough. As it was, the story of the chase abounds in incidents almost too marvelous for belief.

Every point, including St. Paul and Minneapolis, was immediately notified of the robbery, by telegraph, and police officers, detectives and sheriffs posses were sent out after the fleeing bandits, in such numbers that it was thought impossible for any of the outlaws to escape.

Very soon rewards were offered for the apprehension of the desperadoes, which stimulated the already active hunt. The State first proffered $1,000 for the arrest of the six bandits, which offer was changed to $1,000 for each of the gang, dead or alive; $700 was offered by the Northfield bank, and $500 by the Winona & St. Peter railroad.

A posse of fourteen men overtook the bandits on the night of the 11th in a ravine near Shieldsville, and fell back after a fight in which one of the robbers' horses was killed. The dismounted rider was immediately taken up behind one of the others and the band took to the woods. More than 400 men turned out to cut them off. They got into a patch of timber at Lake Elysian and were run out of it the next day, and though the scouting parties increased to a thousand, two days later the robbers had been completely lost. They aimed to go south-west and follow the timber which reaches to the Iowa line, but on the 13th all six were surrounded in the timber near Mankato and all bridges, fords and roads guarded, so that it was thought they could not escape. At two o'clock in the morning four of them came out, ran the guard off Blue Earth bridge and crossed over, and left a regiment of pursuers behind. Next night, two of them, Jesse and Frank James, broke through a picket line on one horse. They were fired upon, and, abandoning the horse, took to a corn-field. While riding double, a ball fired by one of the pursuing posse, struck Frank James in the right knee and passing through, imbedded itself in Jesse's right thigh, producing painful wounds. They stole two grey horses that night from a man named Rockwell and went into Madelia in the morning and bought some bread;

then they took to the prairie and struck out for Dakota. The two grey horses ridden and the overcoats worn by the James Boys left the pursuers an easy means of keeping track of them. Both were so badly hurt and so stiff that when they went to a farm-house and forced the farmer to swap horses with them at the muzzle of the pistol, they had the greatest difficulty in climbing up on a fence to get on the horses' backs. For saddles they had bags stuffed with hay. Yet they got clear away eventually. A posse from Yankton had a fight with them about eight miles out of town, and after having one man wounded, gave it up as a perilous business. The two, soon after, raided a stable, captured two horses, and again outran pursuit.

Near Sioux Falls they met a Dr. Mosher, and made him dress their wounds and change horses and clothing with them. That is the last that was seen of them by their pursuers, they being then in Sioux county, Iowa. They were traced further south to where their horses gave out, and they hired a man to take them on their way in a wagon. Again they were heard of still further down, evidently making for Missouri. Every sheriff and marshal along their line of retreat, was constantly in receipt of letters from Missouri and Kansas, threatening assassination if they arrested the two robbers, and finally the fugitives were lost track of entirely. It is now known that these two, Jesse and Frank James, continued their journey by wagon directly to Mexico.

The other four, Cole, Jim and Bob Younger and Charley Pitts, passed through the town of Mankato on the night of the 13th, and got into the woods west. They robbed a hen-roost, and were just in the act of cooking breakfast, when a posse, who had discovered them, made a charge and drove them out of camp, but without getting sight of them. The worst luck for the robbers was that they had not eaten breakfast, the chickens being left in camp, already picked. Jim Younger afterward said he felt real mean when he was robbing that roost. Large bands of farmers and citizens followed close on their trail, yet the bandits showed such consummate woodcraft, that for two days the pursuers thought the four were only three. One was barefoot, and at every camping-place they left the ground littered with bloody bandages. Finally all trace was lost of them again, but on the morning of the 21st one of the outlaws went to a farm-house, eight miles west of Madelia, and bought some bread and butter. The early hour of his visit and the stiffness of his actions caused a prying young fellow at the house, named Oscar Suborn, to take particular notice of the man. He discovered that the stranger had big revolvers, and that he, with three others, left the road and started west across the country. In less than an hour the boy had taken the news to Madelia. It was yet early in the day, and in fifteen minutes' time, after getting word, Sheriff Glispin and others set out on horseback. For a couple of hours parties were continually starting off, as fast as they could be equipped with arms and horses. Meantime the four stiff and foot-sore wayfarers were trudging along across the prairie toward the timber skirting the Watonwan river. Just at the Hanska slough they were overtaken by the sheriff and advance guard of three or four men, who rode up within one hundred yards and ordered them to surrender. The quartette paid no attention to the summons, but plunging into the slough, waded across. The slough could not be crossed by a horse, so the sheriff had to ride around. The robbers continued to hobble along, as best they could, toward the river, and had made about two miles before the sheriff headed them off They kept straight on for the timber, and the sheriff's party opened on them with rifles. The robbers returned the fire, the bullets whistling so close that the officer and his deputies hastily dismounted and the sheriff's horse was wounded. The robbers got into a belt of timber, and, going through to the other side, saw a hunting party in a wagon, which they made a rush to capture. The men in the wagon instantly presented their shot-guns and the robbers, taking them for pursuers, went back into the brush. It so happened that the patch of timber they had struck was only about five acres in extent, and had bare, open ground all around it. Before they had discovered the disadvantage of their position the people began to flock in from all directions, in wagons, on foot, on horseback, equipped with shot-guns and rifles. They soon established a cordon of one hundred and fifty men around the patch and began shooting into it to drive the game out. As the robbers paid no attention to this, Sheriff Glispen called for volunteers to go in and stir them up. The following went with him: Col. Vaught, Jas. Severson, Ben Rice, Geo. Bradford, Chas. Pomeroy and Capt. Murphy of Madelia. These seven, formed in line a few yards apart and moved cautiously through the brush. The hiding place consisted of about five acres of thick timber, with considerable willow about the marshy parts, but not sufficiently dense to offer any considerable protection.

After the volunteers had advanced into the brush a distance of fifty yards Charley Pitts jumped up in front of Sheriff Glispin and leveled a revolver which exploded almost at the same instant as the sheriff's rifle. The robber ran a couple of rods in a cornering direction and fell dead. The three

Younger Brothers were discovered a moment later, and, as soon as they saw they were in for it, stood up and opened fire. One of the posse was slightly wounded and another had a watch knocked into flinders. Six of the posse returned the volley, the sheriff being busy reloading, and so well directed were their shots that Cole and Jim dropped on the ground, groaning with the pain of shattered bones. Capt. Murphy fired rapidly with a Colt's revolver; Rice and Severson had carbines, while Vaught, Bradford and Pomeroy attacked with double-barrelled shot guns.

While discharging his pistol Capt. Murphy was struck by a 44 calibre ball, but fortunately the bullet hit a pipe in his vest pocket which so spent its force that the only result was a painful bruise. After the first skirmish the bandits retreated a little further which, while hiding from the attacking party, exposed themselves to a large body of men stationed on the north side of the thicket; a volley of gun and pistol shots drove them back again to within twenty yards of the seven volunteers. Cole and Jim were now entirely helpless, in fact Jim was suffering so badly from the wound in his mouth that he had been unable to assist his brothers in defending themselves.

Bob, with one arm hanging broken by his side, stood his ground between the other two, and continued to blaze away with a revolver in his left hand, aiming first at one end of the line, and then at the other, then at the centre, but apparently, trying rather to scare the men off than to hit anybody. One revolver being exhausted, he was handed another. As the posse kept on shooting, however, he finally called out to let up, as the boys were "all shot to pieces." The sheriff made him throw down his pistol and walk forward into the line, when he was secured. Out of all the shots fired at him only one had taken effect, wounding him slightly in the side. The broken arm he had carried all the way from Northfield. The prisoners were secured and taken, with the dead bandit, to Madelia, and placed under the surgical care of Drs. Overholt and Cooley. They confessed that they were the Youngers, but always refused to give any information as to their confederates. Cole had a rifle-ball under the right eye, which paralyzed the optic nerve, and has never yet been extracted. He also had a large revolver bullet in the body and a shot through the thigh, which he got at Northfield, and was wounded altogether in the fight eleven times. Jim was looked upon as a hopeless case by the surgeons. He had eight buckshot and a rifle ball in the body. An ugly wound in the shoulder had been received at Northfield, and he had lost nearly half his jaw by a minie bullet. Bob was the only one who was able to remain on his feet at the surrender. The wound he had received at Northfield had shattered his elbow so as to leave his arm and hand stiff forever. All the old wounds were almost festering for want of attention. After they had rested and had their wounds dressed, every effort was made to get them to tell who were the other two, but without avail. They were always on their guard. One day a man went in to them and said word had just been received that their two comrades, the James Boys, had been overtaken, and one killed and the other wounded and captured.

"How do you know they are the James Boys?" said Cole.

"The wounded man confessed."

"Which one was killed?"

"Frank."

"Which one, I say? The big one or the little one?"

"The big one."

"Did they say anything about us?"

"No."

"Good boy to the last!" — the old guerrilla exclamation to show that a man was game. And that was all that could be got out of them. They were ready to talk about the "big one" and the "little one," but that was all. No names were in their vocabulary. They would not tell who their dead comrades were. The two killed in town were positively identified, however, as Clell Miller and Bill Chadwell. Miller first came into bandit fame in connection with the Corydon bank robbery, and was afterward with the band at the Otterville and Muncie robberies. He was a hard fighter under Quantrill. Chadwell was said to have been driven out of Minnesota for horse-stealing once. His father is reported as having identified his body. Other reports have it that his family belonged in Kansas. The one killed at Madelia was Charles Pitts, or more properly Charles Wells. His chief record was made at Baxter Springs and Otterville.

Worn out, festering with desperate wounds, exposed to terribly inclement weather, camping without blankets in the cold nights of a Northern autumn, and above all, not having had a full meal in two weeks, the Younger brothers gave an exhibition of endurance in this retreat which must be taken as an illustration of unparalleled heroism, which only the most remarkable constitutions could survive.

After the death of Chadwell and Miller they were carried into an empty store on Mill Square, where they remained for some time the object of popular gaze and attention. Chadwell's death wound was located about one

149

inch to the right of the sternum, tearing away his lungs and passing out at the back below the shoulder-blade. Clell Miller was struck by a minie ball which penetrated the left breast just below the clavicle. Besides this wound he was struck in the shoulder and face by a charge of shot, evidently fired from Stacy's gun.

The captured Younger brothers were taken to Madelia where they received surgical attention at the Flanders House. Cole and Jim were placed in the same bed, while Bob was accommodated in another room. Their wounds, though of a serious character, were pronounced not dangerous. During their stay at Madelia they were daily visited by hundreds of men and women, many of the latter bringing testimonials of regard for the heroism displayed by the stricken bandits. Cole Younger, though badly wounded, received his visitors in a most affable manner, and all the brothers demeaned themselves in such a way as to win the respect of all who called, each having some kind and cheerful words with which to answer even impertinent questions. After some telegraphic correspondence between the Governor, who was attending the Centennial Exposition at Philadelphia, and Capt. Macy, his secretary, an order was received to place the prisoners in the county jail at Faribault, the county seat of Rice county, and to convey the remains of the dead bandit to St. Paul, which was accordingly done, the dead body being given to the Surgeon General of the State for embalming.

After the Younger brothers were incarcerated in jail, several detectives from northwestern cities, and James McDonough, chief of the St. Louis police, met in St. Paul and went by special train to Faribault to interview and identify the prisoners. The entertaining trio had so far recovered as to be able to receive their visitors in excellent style. When the party entered the jail they found Cole and Bob smoking and reading the daily papers. Jim, however, was still suffering severely from the wound in his mouth. A very interesting conversation of more than two hours duration was had, in which no information was gleaned of importance.

Miss Retta Younger, a sister of the bandits, and a lovely lady of refinement and unexceptionable character, seventeen years of age, visited the brothers directly after their capture; her grief and refined deportment gained for her the sympathy of every one, and the impression she created was of the most favorable nature. Mrs. Fannie Twyman, an aunt, was also with the brothers, and she, too, met with the highest esteem from the citizens of Faribault.

The Grand Jury that was summoned returned four bills of indictment against the captured bandits, and Cole Younger was specially charged with murdering the Norwegian, which bill was found on the testimony of two witnesses, who swore they saw Cole commit the deed.

On the 7th of November the district court convened, Judge Lord presiding. The prosecution was represented by the prosecuting attorney, George N. Baxter, Esq., and the prisoners had for their counsel Thomas Rutledge, Esq., of Medalia, and Bachelder & Buckham, of Faribault. It was the intention of the Youngers to plead "not guilty," but when they were forced to stand a trial on the charge of murder in the first degree, in order to avoid capital punishment, they entered a plea of "guilty." Had the charge of murder been confined to Haywood, the brothers would have stood a trial, because they could have proved, positively, that neither of them fired the fatal ball at the cashier, and as a conviction could only have resulted in a life sentence, they could have afforded to take the chances.

After entering the plea of "guilty," Judge Lord ordered the prisoners to stand up and receive sentence. The order of the court was that each of the brothers should be confined in the State penitentiary at Stillwater, for the period of their natural lives. When this sentence was pronounced, the young and beautiful sister almost fainted; recovering her strength she fell on Cole's neck and gave expression to such intense suffering of mind that nearly every one in the court-room was moved to tears. Sheriff Barton could hardly persuade the devoted sister to abate her manifestations of grief. Thenceforth she did not leave her brothers until they were conveyed to the penitentiary, to which place she accompanied them, and when circumstances compelled them to part she was fairly overwhelmed with sorrow. Her love was fully reciprocated by the erring brothers, and such an attachment could not fail in creating a strong bond of sympathy between the citizens and the unhappy sister.

# A PROPOSITION TO MURDER JIM YOUNGER.

The wound received by Jim Younger in the fight at Northfield, while in no sense dangerous, was the most unfortunate blow that struck the bandits. The hemorrhage from his shattered mouth was so profuse, that a trail of blood was left behind him, easily distinguishable by the pursuers. Two miles from Dundas and a little more than one hour after fleeing out of Northfield, the bandits stopped at a farmhouse and, borrowing a pail, they repaired to the spring where the wounded men were bathed and every effort was made to stay the bleeding of Jim's mouth. Water, however, seemed to aggravate the difficulty. His linen duster was torn into bandages, but the wound being difficult to bind, the cloths were soon saturated and had to be thrown away, furnishing another indication of the retreat. The hemorrhage continued until Jim became so weak that it was necessary for Cole and Bob to ride beside and support him in the saddle. This retarded the fugitives for several days, while the woods were fairly swarming with their pursuers.

On the 13th, while the party were hobbling through swamps and finding every avenue guarded, Jesse James — so it is reported by an ex-guerrilla who has maintained relations, for many years, with the James and Younger Boys — spoke to Cole Younger about as follows:

"Cole, we are in a bad fix, and there is only one way out, so it appears to me. Our trail is so plain that a blind man can follow it; if we are surrounded it means death to us all. It's a terrible thought, but the circumstances are terrible. Jim cannot live; he is almost dead now. We can't continue our retreat with him; we can't hide, and to carry him along with us will only result in certain death to the whole party. None of us could consent to his falling into the hands of the men now hunting us, and therefore, everything considered, I think it would be right to dispose of him, thereby ending his sufferings which must finally end in his death; we could then travel faster and, I think, escape."

Cole and Bob Younger looked at Jesse for some moments before replying; that they were mad there could be no doubt. Finally Cole replied:

"Jesse James, you are a cold-hearted villain; a very monster that I can never again associate with. Now, here, let us separate. If Frank (James)

152

shares your sentiments, or Charley (Pitts) entertains such a wish, take your own route and never meet me again. To kill my brother! why, I'll stay by him till he dies and then I'll carry his dead body with me as long as my strength makes it possible."

Frank James expressed some dissent from Jesse's proposition, as did Charley Pitts, but it was finally agreed that the James Brothers should go their way, as Cole and Bob could no longer endure Jesse's company. It was thus the party separated, Pitts remaining with the Youngers.

The fraternal devotion of Cole and Bob Younger never needed stronger manifestation. They did remain with their stricken brother; carried him through swamps, over streams, into the deepest recesses of the forest, and when their own wounds, deep and terrible, had become so festered, and their limbs stiffened, that further progress was impossible, they laid their precious charge down tenderly upon the leaves and there remained, exhausted and prostrate, until the capture was consummated. What noble hearts to be concealed beneath the exterior of these outlaws!

# AN INTERESTING CORRESPONDENCE FROM COLE YOUNGER.

Since the arrest of the Younger Brothers more than a hundred attempts have been made by book-writers, to secure a history of the noted outlaws from their own lips. These efforts were made, principally, by correspondence, but not a few sanguine authors and reporters have visited the penitentiary and used all the force of persuasive eloquence, and proffered money considerations to the Youngers for a recital of their interesting exploits. The manner in which these influences resulted, is told in Cole Younger's first letter, which is given in full herewith.

Being acquainted with so many of the old chums of the Younger and James Boys, who knew my purpose of preparing a history of the famous bandits, time and again I was assured by them, that a letter to Cole Younger would be answered. At length I wrote to warden Reed, of the Minnesota penitentiary, requesting his influence with the Youngers, inducing them to write to me. In due time the warden replied that the inflexible rule of the three brothers was to make no reply to any communication indicating a purpose like the one I manifested. But being more especially desirous of demonstrating my disposition not to do the incarcerated brothers any intentional injustice, I wrote, addressing each of the Youngers in person, acquainting them with my purpose and requesting an answer.

The reply received is as follows:

Stillwater, Minn., Oct. 20, 1880.

J. W. Buel, Esq.,

Dear Sir: — Your letter was received some days ago. The reason I did not answer soon was owing to the fact that when we were first captured, I received a great many letters from different parties all wanting to write a history of my life, and to be just to all I replied to none. But as yours is the only letter of the kind I have received for a long time, I have concluded to write you.

Without intending the least disrespect, permit me to say: positively, I will have nothing to do with writing a history of any kind. Now if you have determined to prepare such a history — and I presume you have — I will aid you only so much as to refer you to those who served with me in the Lost Cause. You will find the names of all of them in Edwards' book, entitled "Shelby and his Men." Most of these men still live in Jackson, Cass, Johnson and Lafayette counties; I am willing to abide by any statement they may make concerning me.

As for anything since the war, a true statement would fall flat. I am aware that my name has been connected with all the bank robberies in the country; but positively I had nothing to do with any one of them. I look upon my life since the war as a blank, and will never say anything to make it appear otherwise. The world may believe as it pleases.

I presume that you are a professional writer, and, like many others, have been led to believe by sensational newspaper reports, that there are historical facts sufficient connected with my life to make an interesting book, but it is a mistake, unless nine-tenths of the matter is fiction.

As to the facts connected with my career in Minnesota, I will refer you to those equally well qualified to give them; the sheriff of Watawan county. Sheriff Barton of Rice county, the clerks in the bank at Northfield, and Warden Reed, of this place. They could give you all the facts you could possibly get from me. I should not object to a visit from you, but will tell you in advance that I will give none of the details of my past life. I would as willingly assist you as any person, but my answer is alike to all. I am one who never insinuates; I use nothing but plain words. As for the names of the two men who were with us at Northfield, they will ever remain unknown to the world, so far as I am concerned.

Very respectfully,

T. C. Younger.

This letter, while affording little information or encouragement, was, nevertheless, so respectful in its tone, that I immediately answered it at considerable length, repeating my earnest desire to do all the brothers justice, which I feared could not be done without some necessary statements from them. I proffered space in my book for any epistolary vindication they might choose to make, and then sought to impress upon them the importance of accepting the offer. I referred to a great many matters of interest to the public and gave my assurance (which I trust has in no sense been violated) that I should treat them in the fairest possible manner, but that in the absence of positive testimony the circumstantial evidence I was compelled to use might do them grievous wrong, a result I was exceedingly anxious to avoid. To this communication I received the following courteous and very gratifying reply:

Stillwater, Minn., Oct. 31, 1880.

J W. Buel, Esq.,

My Dear Sir: — Your letter of the 24th inst. came to hand in due time, and through the kindness of Warden Reed I am permitted to answer the same. I am glad to learn that you receive my refusal to assist in preparing a history of my life in the spirit I intended, for I am sure I meant no discourtesy.

I observe by your letter that you still entertain the opinion that there are historical facts connected with my life worthy of record in print, but I assure you that such an idea is erroneous, at least that is my opinion. You had better confine yourself to the war record as long as possible, for when you leave that it is like launching a boat into the ocean without a rudder, compass, or lighthouse, the voyage becomes doubtful.

You announce your desire to question me concerning the James Boys. Of course I have no idea of the nature of your questions, but if they involve information respecting what they have been accused of since the war, then I will make no answer. If either of them ever trusted me with a secret, there is no power on earth that could induce me to betray that trust — nor that of any one else. No matter how much I might condemn the act, or how bitter enemies we might have become afterward, it would be all the same.

You speak of seeing George Shepherd. He surely told you that Jess (Jesse James) and I were never friends, for he knows all that prevented us from settling our difficulty, in '72, on the field of honor, was the intercession of Frank and others. Frank and I were always good friends, but we have seen little of each other since the war. He was a brave soldier, a true friend and a gentleman. Now don't obtain the idea from this that I wish to leave an impression that Jess was all to blame in our differences, or who was in fault, he or myself I am sure I would not lay all the burden of blame upon him now, as he is dead or worse than dead. I never, for a moment doubted the fact of George Shepherd shooting him.

You speak of writing Shepherd's history. I have no doubt that he had more ups and downs during the war than any other man connected with Quantrill. I have been in some very close places with him myself We were together most of the time until the fall of '63, when I took my company to Louisiana. I have not seen him but twice since the first of January, 1866, and then but a short time. I know nothing of his career since the war. He is the quickest man on earth; a stranger might take him for a coward, but in that he would be mistaken, for Shepherd is a brave man. You have, probably, learned that he is no friend of mine, or I have been told by others he was not, but I have no idea what he has against me. I was very much surprised to learn that he was trying to injure me after I was down, unless he thinks I am like Conrad, in Byron's Corsair:

"Fallen too low to fear another fall."

That may be true, but I hate to think of being assisted in my fall by one with whom I have periled my life, and for the same cause. If he thinks he has grounds for becoming an enemy of mine, it must be the result of newspaper reports, for if he was connected with any of the bank robberies, he knows I was not present, and if he was not there, what right has he to declare who was? But enough of this, for I still wish him well, according to his deserts.

I am very thankful for your kind offer to let me have space in your book, should I wish to say anything in my own defense. I have nothing to say, unless it would be a request, using the language of Othello:

"Speak of me as I am, nothing extenuate
Nor set down aught in malice."

If you choose you may use a letter I wrote to my brother-in-law, Lycurgas Jones, of Cass county, in November, 1874, and published in the Pleasant Hill Review.

You request my opinion of all the books pretending to record the incidents of my life. With the exception of Maj. Edwards' history all the others are humbugs.

In relation to Walley I will say: if I were what the world paints me, there could be no excuse except cowardice for my neglect to kill him. During the war I did everything in my power to get hold of him, but failed. I went into Kansas City, Independence, and other places, when they were garrisoned by from three hundred to a thousand Federals, in search of Walley, but could never find him.

When I returned home from the war I found a widowed mother, with little children to take care of, and to be able to assist them, I buried everything connected with the war. But I was forced to leave home again, and then I could have killed Walley nearly any time, but only by assassination — slipping to his house and shooting him through the window. Some people might have perpetrated such a deed, but I could never pollute my soul with such a crime. I challenged him during the war, but he paid no attention to it, hiding from me all the time in the most cowardly manner. I could not shoot him like a dog, especially when I knew he had a wife and children.

There is one thing I wish you would note respecting the character of the guerrillas. It is the popular impression among people of other States that we were sneak-thieves like the bushwhackers of Virginia, Tennessee and Arkansas, who hid in the mountains and sallied out during the night to kill old men and rob defenceless women and children. This you know is a fallacy and an unjust stigma upon the guerrillas.

If you wish to know how I treated citizens during the most furious days of the war, I will refer you, for that information, to the Union men in Cass, Jackson or Gentry counties, or personally, to Martin O. Jones, or Sampson, the Jew. in Independence. You are acquainted in Jackson county and know these men to be honorable and prominent Unionists. The only bulldozing I ever did was in making men who remained at home during the winter of '62 get wood for the women and children; for the wives of Union as well as Confederate soldiers.

The question has been asked thousands of times: "Why have the Youngers been protected and befriended so long by the people in the western counties of Missouri?" There are two reasons: First, because they never believed we were guilty of the crimes charged upon us; and second because I befriended them during the war. At the most critical period of the great strife, in 1862, we had five different farms in Cass and Jackson counties, with corn cribs full of corn. When food became difficult to obtain, I told all the poor people to help themselves and take what corn they needed, without charge. I made no distinction then between Federals and Confederates. Wash. Sallie was at the county farm, adjoining ours, at the time; you probably know him; he will confirm what I say, and will tell you that we had five thousand bushels of corn at that farm which I distributed to the poor without distinction. There are many mothers, wives and daughters still living who will credit me with an honorable part during the war, and of risking my life in the defense of their fathers, husbands and brothers. I never, under any circumstances, refused to aid a friend, regardless of political predilections, a claim which not one of my old comrades will dispute.

I have written you more than I intended when I commenced. I will ask you to pay no attention to what I have said, until all my assertions are corroborated by other sources, satisfactory to yourself; then use the facts as you deem proper.

I was a soldier and fought to hurt, but I never molested non-combatants.

T. C. Younger.

# A PERSONAL INTERVIEW WITH COLE YOUNGER.

The lengthy communication of October 31st, from Cole Younger, determined me upon a visit to Stillwater for the purpose of having a personal interview with the noted brothers, and in accordance with this decision I left St. Louis on the 5th of November and arrived at my destination on the morning of the 7th. After introducing myself to Warden Reed, that very affable prison official conducted me at once to a reception-room where, after a very short wait, Cole, Jim and Bob Younger walked in, by whom I was greeted very cordially. My first tacit observation was, "did I ever see three finer looking men?" Cole is the largest, being about six feet three inches in height, but all the brothers measure considerably over six feet, and their bodies are knit together with that smooth compactness which indicates the strength of steel. They were models of form, and if I were a woman I should have no hesitancy in pronouncing each of them decidedly handsome. But better than all this, they bear themselves like perfect gentlemen and never fail, so I am told, in producing the most favorable impression upon all their visitors, of whom they have not a few. Cole is the spokesman of the trio, and in the beginning it is well to admit that a shrewder questioner or witness never made use of brain and tongue than he. Physiology and phrenology both unite in adapting him for the bar; as a lawyer he would undoubtedly have made a phenomenal success; the magnificence of his physique and sharp wits, which manifest themselves in cunning speech and comprehension and quick ideas, leave no doubt of what his career as an advocate would have been. His first words were:

"Well, I learn from your letters that you have decided to write a history of the James and Younger Boys."

"Yes," said I, "such has been my purpose for some years past, and much of the work is already completed; what remains to be finished I have left until some very necessary information may be gathered from you."

"I am very glad to see you," he responded; "but I fear that resolutions, which I have long since taken, will prevent me from making your visit a profitable one."

I replied: "The object of my visit does not contemplate the forging of secrets from your breast; from the tenor of your communications I judged your character; that there were many things which were with you inviolably sacred; I was also assured that no trust confided to your keeping would ever be violated. Upon such subjects I have no wish to question you, but only upon such matters as regard yourself, the war and other things, to speak of which you will not compromise your manhood or honor."

" I cannot see what interest, then, an interview with me would possess more than that with any other of the ex-guerrillas, many of whom are still living," he replied.

I answered: "The relations to the public are different, and then there are some things of which you might honorably speak, chiefly concerning yourself, that would be of special interest to the thousands who have read of your exploits."

"Well," said he, "propound your questions, and what I can conscientiously answer I will, but when you tread upon sacred grounds I shall be quick to inform you."

Q. In the first place explain, if you can, some of the causes which produced the guerrillas of Missouri.

A. It would require a history to answer that question properly. The people of western Missouri are, in some respects, very peculiar. We will take Jackson county (where I was born) for instance. In that section the people seemed to be born fighters, the instinct being inherited from a long line of ancestors. It would have been a good idea if, in your book, you had given a short history of that county; the facts might easily be collected in Independence where many old settlers still reside, who are familiar with some of the bitter antagonisms which distinguished the early settlement of that district.

Joe Smith and Brigham Young laid out Independence, but very soon thereafter enough citizens of the county collected to drive them off, after several stubborn fights. The Mormons withdrew from the State and settled their community at Nauvoo, Illinois, but in a few years afterward about fifty of them again came into Missouri and settled in Platte county. They had scarcely established themselves, however, before another company of Jackson county citizens, chiefly from around Independence, organized to drive them off. Among these determined citizens were Richard Fristoe, my grandfather. Wood Nolen, Smallwood Nolen and Sam Owens. While crossing the river in a hand-ferry-boat, the ferryman, who had been bribed by the Mormons, succeeded in turning the boat over midway in the

Missouri river. A large number were drowned, but the four I have mentioned succeeded in swimming ashore.

Independence was, for a long time previous to the war with Mexico, headquarters for Mexican freighters. The freight passing between Mexico and Missouri was carried on pack-mules, many Jackson county men being engaged in that business.

It was in Jackson county chiefly, also, that Col. Doniphan recruited his famous regiment for the Mexican war and made that wonderful march known in history as De rando del murato, (the journey of death). After subduing New Mexico, Doniphan marched to Chihuahua, which then had 40,000 inhabitants, and raised the United States flag over the citadel; and from this latter place he continued his march to the Gulf of Mexico.

Independence became also the headquarters and fitting-out post of the Forty-Niners when the great pilgrimage to California began. Majors Russell and Waddell, the greatest overland freighters the world has ever produced, lived in Independence.

In the war of 1856 Jackson county, and the settlement about Independence especially, was more largely represented, perhaps, than any other section. This diabolical war, distinguished by the most atrocious cruelties the conqueror can inflict upon his captive, prepared the way, and created the guerrilla in 1862. Natural fighters, conducting a war of spoliation and reprisal, — through the brush, — trained to quick sorties and deadly ambuscades, how easily they drifted as their instincts inclined, and became guerrillas by an irresistible combination of circumstances, such as I have explained.

Q. Your answer is very comprehensive and interesting. Now, will you be kind enough to tell me what finally became of the "Black Flag" which Quantrill carried? Geo. Shepherd gave me a very interesting history of that flag, which I shall relate in my book, but he was unable to tell me what eventually became of that ominous symbol.

A. Jim Lane carried a black flag until the fall of 1863, when we captured it, and sometime afterward we sent it to Sterling Price. I think both flags were subsequently cut up and made into over-shirts which some of the boys wore.

Q. Do you know where Quantrill is buried?

A. He sleeps in the Catholic grave-yard at Louisville, Ky.

Q. Do you know whether or not Jesse and Frank James are full brothers?

A. Surely their mother is the same, and I presume their father was also the same, but he was dead long before I knew the family.

Q. Will you explain the causes and circumstances which led you to Northfield; also, explain, please, how you became separated from the two comrades who succeeded in escaping? I have been told that the shooting of Jim Younger, in the mouth, caused such profuse hemorrhage that the pursuers could trail you by the blood; that one of the two who escaped insisted on killing Jim in order to destroy the trail, and that it was this proposition which caused the separation.

A. Positively, I will have nothing to do with writing or furnishing any information concerning the Northfield robbery, or any other robbery. I do not say this through any unkindness; I have made the same reply to life-long friends, among whom were two brothers-in-law. I should say the same to sister Retta, whom I love better than all the world, if she should ask me the question.

Q. How long was each of you in the surgeon's care after your capture?

A. Jim and I are still receiving surgical attention, and will be the remainder of our lives.

Q. How often have you and your brothers been wounded?

A. I have been wounded altogether twenty times; eleven of these wounds were received at Northfield. Jim was wounded four times at Northfield, and six times in all. Bob was never wounded until the pursuit in Minnesota, where he was struck three times.

Q. Can you tell me who was in command at Independence and issued the order that thereafter guerrillas taken by capture would not be treated like ordinary prisoners of war? Shepherd says he is not certain, but thinks it was Maj. Blunt.

A. It was Jennison, Colonel of the 15th Kansas cavalry.

Q. What are your respective duties in the penitentiary?

A. We have no special duties. Jim and I being on the hospital list do very little, while Bob performs various duties. I occupy much of my time in theological studies for which I have a natural inclination. It was the earliest desire of my parents to prepare me for the ministry, but the horrors of war, the murder of my father, and the outrages perpetrated upon my poor old mother, my sisters and brothers, destroyed our hopes so effectually that none of us could be prepared for any duty in life except revenge.

The tear which stole into Cole's eye told how much he suffered in the remembrance of those sorrow-laden days when war drove happiness eternally from the Younger household. Out of deference to that honorable feeling, I could not question him further upon such an extremely unpleasant subject.

Q. How do you regard your treatment in the prison?

A. I will say that since our capture we have met with uniform kindness, and while in the penitentiary our relations with the officers have been cordially pleasant, and for their considerate and kind disposition we feel profoundly grateful. There has never been so much as a hard thought between us. While I think of it, I should like to ask a favor: In your last letter you seemed to intimate that I had self in view by referring to the liberality with which I distributed corn to the poor in 1862-3. Now the favor I ask is this: In the first place, many of my old comrades are married and settled down in Missouri, where they are living peaceful lives. I want it understood that all these men fought for principle, not for plunder, and that they were true-hearted, honorable soldiers, fighting for what they esteemed was a righteous cause. In relation to me giving corn, and also pork and beef, to the poor during that hard winter, when food was so difficult to obtain, I will only say that I was following an example set by my blessed and sainted mother, whose charitable heart never failed to respond to distress. These facts I desire you to make understood in your book.

Q. How much land did your father own at the time of his assassination?

A. He had 3,500 acres, a greater part of which was under cultivation, with barns, houses, etc. All this property went with the ravages of the war. My part has long since been spent in keeping out of the clutches of mobs.

I thanked Cole and his brothers for the marked kindness they had shown me, and after again explaining the possible necessities, owing to conflicting and current errors, of my connecting them with crimes of which they were perhaps as innocent as myself, we shook hands cordially and I withdrew.

After my return to St. Louis I instituted inquiries, by letter, in order to receive a denial or corroboration of Cole Younger's statements, respecting his liberality and conduct during the war. I communicated with several Union men, all of whom, while pronouncing Cole a desperate fighter, yet accorded him full credit for his magnanimity in helping the poor, relieving distress and affording every possible protection to women and children, regardless of political sentiments.

# HOW A DUEL TO THE DEATH WAS PREVENTED.

The position taken by Cole Younger with respect to talking upon incidents subsequent to the war, prevented me from obtaining all the information I so earnestly sought. That portion of his letter referring to a proposed duel between himself and Jesse James, which was prevented by Frank James and others, possessed for me considerable interest, and to learn the facts leading to so desperate a conclusion, I again visited Kansas City and secured an interview with George Shepherd, in which he gave me the entire story, as follows:

"When I left Kentucky after the expiration of my term of imprisonment, I visited my sister at Lee's Summit, in Jackson county. On the day following my return, which I think was early in 1872, Jesse James, hearing of my arrival, came ever to see me. In the course of our conversation he said:

"'George, I saw Cole yesterday.'

"'Well, how is he and what did he say?' I replied.

"Jess looked a little serious, and responded:

"'He told me to tell you that under no circumstances did he ever want to see you again; Cole is bitter against you, George.'

"My answer was: 'I don't know what he has against me, but you can tell him he need not trouble about meeting me, or put himself in a place to see me if he don't want to.'

"Two days after this meeting I went up to see old Silas Hudspeth, near the Six Mile district. I was ignorant of the cause which had disturbed Cole's friendly relations with me, and I was determined not to make any special effort to find out. I reached Hudspeth's house some time after dark, and riding up to the front gate, I called out, 'hello!' The old man came to the door and I told him who I was; he drew back a step and spoke to some one in the house, after which he invited me to get down and come in. Just as I stepped on the porch. Cole, speaking from the inside where I could not see him, said: 'Shepherd, I am in here, you ain't afraid, are you?'

"I replied: 'That's all right; of course I'm not afraid,' and then I walked in. Cole was sitting in a chair in one corner of the room, and I at once saw he had a pistol. We spoke very little, confining our conversation to the old man. When it came bedtime, Hudspeth told us to occupy a bed together.

After we undressed and lay down, I saw Cole reach up under his pillow and draw out a pistol which he put beside him under the cover. Not to be taken unawares, I at once grasped my own pistol and shoved it down under the covers beside me. To save my life I couldn't think of any reason Cole could have for becoming an enemy. We talked very little, but just lay there watching each other. He was behind and I on the front side of the bed, and during the entire night we looked into each others' eyes, and never once moved. It was the most wretched eight hours I ever spent in my life. Of course, I wouldn't percipitate a fight or shoot him without cause, so I waited, determined only to protect my own life. Singularly enough. Cole was actuated by the same ideas.

"As quickly as dawn began to appear, I got up and dressed, as did also Cole; he never for one instant took his eye off me, but followed my actions and kept within an arm's length of me continually. You can imagine, how peculiar I felt; if I could have concluded what produced his anger, then I would have known how to act, but my ignorance of the cause of his offense, and finding him apparently watching for a chance to kill me so dead, instantly, that I could not return his fire, made me wretched beyond expression.

"Old man Hudspeth finally got up and prepared breakfast, he being an old bachelor, and when we sat down to the table. Cole broke our suspense by remarking to me: 'I heard, yesterday, that you intended to kill me on sight; have you lost your nerve?'

"My surprise, I know, was indicated by my looks. I replied: 'In the name of God, who told you such a thing? Why, I never for a moment even harbored a hard feeling toward you. Who told you that, Cole?'

"'I met Jess yesterday, and he told me that you sent that message to me by him,' Cole responded.

"Then the whole thing appeared plain to me. I had learned at Lee's Summit that Jesse James bore Cole a mortal hatred, and he had become a bearer of exasperating falsehoods between us so as to provoke a quarrel that would end in one of us being shot.

"I told Cole how infamous the he was and then related to him what Jess had told me, conveying his, (Cole's) wishes not to see me. Of course, full explanations followed, and then Cole was one of the maddest men I ever saw. He despised Jesse James, but the primary cause of the difficulty between them was never told me.

"We remained at Hudspeth's house until nearly ten o'clock in the morning, and as we were getting ready to leave, Jesse and Frank James and John Younger came riding up the road and hitched their horses to the fence with the intention of coming in; Cole, however, met them and I saw at once that there was a cloud of difficulty in the horizon several times bigger than a man's hand. As they advanced toward each other. Cole drew his pistol and threw the muzzle directly in Jess' face, calling him, at the same time, all the abusive names he could think of. We finally parted them, or rather, quieted Cole, after which Jess and Frank rode off in one direction, while Cole and John Younger took the opposite.

"Shortly after this occurrence the James Boys went to Louisiana and were followed, in a few weeks afterward, by Cole and John Younger. I don't think the Youngers knew where the James Boys had gone. Anyhow, Cole and John decided to visit John Jarrette, who was living at a point in Louisiana I don't care to mention. As they came riding toward Jarrette's house, it chanced that the James Boys were there and saw them. Immediately Jess and Frank seized their double-barreled shot-guns and, running out of the house, they took positions behind two trees, as if intending to murder the Youngers. Cole saw and recognized, them. Now, Frank James was a friend of Cole's and he did everything in his power to quiet Jess, but the reason he seized his gun and joined Jess, was in order to help his brother if both Cole and John should attack him.

"There never was a more fearless man than Cole Younger, and Jesse James knew that if he tackled him, it meant a fight to the death. Cole, with his pistol in hand, dared Jess to fire at him, and then gave him a challenge to come out from behind the tree and fight him at five or ten paces with shot-guns or pistols. Jess showed some disposition to accept the challenge, and it did look as though there would be one or more funerals in the woods, maybe, before dark. Fortunately for both of them, Frank James, John Younger and Jarrette succeeded in preventing what would have been a deadly meeting."

Being un-able to obtain an answer to the question from the Youngers themselves, after the conclusion of Shepherd's story, the writer asked him for an opinion respecting the guilt or innocence of the Youngers as to the charges of bank and train robberies made against them.

His reply was as follows: "Speaking of Cole Younger, I have no hesitancy in saying that, outside of the affair at Northfield, I don't believe he was ever connected with the James Boys, or that he ever participated in any of the robberies. This much, I know; I have heard the James Brothers propose raids of that kind to him, asking him to join them, and every time, in my presence, he not only refused absolutely, but manifested a feeling of insult and pronounced the schemes outrageous, even going so far as to express a hope, that if they perpetrated such robberies, they would be caught and punished as they deserved. I also know that he was not at Russellville. As to the Otterville train robbery, I am aware that Hobbs Kerry's confession, which seemed to be corroborated by the attack at Northfield afterward, surrounds Cole by very strong circumstantial evidence of guilt, but I have been told by one who knew all the parties implicated in the robbery, that Cole was not there."

The writer then asked the further question:

"Tell me, please, if Cole and Jesse James have been such implacable enemies, how it happened that they joined together in the scheme to rob the Northfield bank?"

Shepherd made response: "Well, that is a question which I should like as much to have answered, maybe more so than yourself. I feel certain, from facts learned since that attack, that they were never reconciled to each other, and how it happened they rode together in that raid, puzzles me more than I can tell you. I mean to find out, some time, however."

# ATTEMPTS TO LIBERATE THE YOUNGER BROTHERS.

Considering the cunning and notoriety of the imprisoned bandits, it is not astonishing that attempts to liberate them should be made. More than two score of the old guerrillas are still living, all men of remarkable courage, and their devotion to one another recognizes, in a measure, the binding obligation of the Black Oath, though the desperate days of its constant use are over. Aside from the strong bands of friendship forged by the direful necessities of war, in which Cole Younger was such a consummate hero, there are other considerations which create a sympathy on the part of hundreds of western Missourians for the incarcerated outlaws. It has been reported, but upon authority which, to say the least, is far from conclusive, that a large sum of money was raised by voluntary contributions for the purpose' of bribing the penitentiary officials to permit an escape of the Youngers; one publication fixes the sum so raised at $70,000, but this is too absurd for any rational person to credit.

Some time in 1877 there was an attempt to release the bandits, but it was so clumsily arranged that there is grave doubt if either the Youngers or the prison authorities ever knew of it. The circumstances, which were published about two years ago in a country paper of north-west Missouri, are, as far as remembered, about as follows: Canvassing as a book-agent for "Edwards' Noted Guerrillas" in the north-western part of Missouri, was an ex-guerrilla whose admiration for Cole Younger amounted to infatuation. He placed so much confidence in the ability of the Youngers to effect an escape from any place of confinement, that it was his frequent boast, to those about him, that the Stillwater officers would very soon be treated to a first-class surprise. But when he saw month after month pass away, with the Youngers still deprived of their liberty, he began to consider the means employed to hold them in captivity. In the latter part of 1877, this enthusiastic admirer of his imprisoned comrade chanced to meet a friend who had also marched under Quantrill's black flag, and was then pursuing a peripatetic calling, but not for philosophic purposes. The two, after exchanging the formulas of friendship, very naturally began a discussion of the Youngers' imprisonment. They remained together for several days, devoting their entire time to propositions looking to a release of their friends.

After proposing and debating more than a score of schemes, the two anxious ex-guerrillas concluded to adopt some bold measure, as they could depend upon the Youngers in every emergency however dangerous. Their decision was that each should leave Missouri and proceed directly to Minnesota; they were to assume false names; appear as strangers to each other, and then commit some crime that would cause them to serve a short term in the penitentiary. The most reliable friends of the Youngers were made acquainted with the plan intended to be put into execution, and were advised to hold themselves in readiness to lend any necessary assistance. The faithful couple, who were ready to suffer any punishment, if there were any hope it would result in the liberation of their captive comrades, went into Minnesota by different routes, and as per their arrangement, one stole a watch and the other purloined some article of small value. The result of their thefts, however, was far from what they expected. The one who took the watch was sentenced to the penitentiary for one year, while the other, though very anxious to accompany his companion, and making no defense whatever, was committed to the county jail for a short period. This unforeseen termination of their trials completely destroyed the purposes of the scheme. The one sentenced to the penitentiary found, upon entering that penal institution, that there were no possible means of communicating with the Youngers, owing to the rigid discipline of the prison, and he was, therefore, forced to serve his full time, at hard labor, without even the consolation of conveying his well-intended purpose to his captive friends. After his liberation from the penitentiary, the ex-guerrilla returned to the same county from whence he departed with a determination to release Cole Younger, especially, and sorrowfully repeated the result of his abortive attempt; no persuasion, however, could induce him to explain the details of his scheme, the reason evidently being, because of an anticipation that it would some day be renewed with better success.